KING AND COMMONS
1660–1832

KING AND COMMONS
1660–1832

BY

BETTY KEMP, M.A.
*Fellow of St. Hugh's College,
Oxford*

62442

LONDON
MACMILLAN & CO LTD
NEW YORK · ST MARTIN'S PRESS
1965

First Edition 1957
Reprinted 1959, 1965

MACMILLAN AND COMPANY LIMITED
Little Essex Street London WC 2
also Bombay Calcutta Madras Melbourne

THE MACMILLAN COMPANY OF CANADA LIMITED
70 Bond Street Toronto 2

ST MARTIN'S PRESS INC
175 Fifth Avenue New York 10010 NY

PRINTED IN GREAT BRITAIN

TO
LEWIS NAMIER

PREFACE

I AM very grateful to Mr. Richard Pares, Fellow of All Souls College, Oxford, for reading this book at an early typescript stage, and to Dr. H. G. Hanbury, Vinerian Professor of English Law in the University of Oxford, for reading the pages which deal with clauses 24 and 25 of the Succession to the Crown Act of 1707.

CONTENTS

CHAPTER I

INTRODUCTION

THE relationship between King and Commons, which links two branches of a tripartite legislature, also links a permanent head of the executive and a changing, elected body which, though depending for its existence on the King's will, yet has part in validating at least some of his acts. It is clear that, not only in the period 1660–1832, but at every stage in the development of this relationship, the King influenced, to a greater or lesser extent, both the composition and the conduct of the Commons : by pressure at elections and by attention to his supporters in the House. But since the King's influence, however great, was never absolute, every period poses the same question : to what extent, and with what success, did the King woo the Commons he had caused to be summoned ? The question is complicated by the fact that one of the most effective ways of wooing has often been to plant King's servants in the Commons, or to bestow crown offices on members of the Commons, so that some members of the House looked to two masters. The Commons as a whole inevitably opposed this infiltration until, by process of time, it seemed harmless, and they opposed it either by trying to prevent it altogether or by trying to limit it. Yet, without it, co-operation between King and Commons could hardly have existed.

In the course of the period between the Restoration and the Reform Act there was achieved, and for a time maintained, a constitutional balance of power between a King who was still powerful and a House of Commons which was newly powerful. The King's wooing of the Commons in this period was of pre-eminent importance because, since both were strong and neither was certainly sovereign, co-operation between them was essential. The fight between King and Commons in the seventeenth century restricted the King's powers without making the Commons his master, even in the financial sphere, and to contemporaries at least it was remarkable that the Commons remained so long content with an incomplete victory. Because they did, the relationship between King and Commons in the eighteenth century was, for the first and last time, a balanced relationship between two more or less equal partners, of which the second did not owe all its powers, nor indeed entirely its existence, to the first.

Constitutional theory supported the relationship, for it taught that a balance between independent and strong powers prevented tyranny. And so perhaps it did. For when the balance between King and Commons was at length undermined, the undermining was due, not to the growth in power of one at the expense of the other, but to the advent of a freer and more independent electorate, no longer seriously influenced by the King and not checked or balanced by any other power. The electorate, more or less influenced, had of course always chosen the House of Commons, but in the eighteenth century the choice had been made, on the whole, in the interests of the King, and attempts by constituencies to do more than elect — for example, to instruct or exact promises from their members at the time of election, or to bind them later to a particular policy — were generally regarded as unconstitutional and had little success. These attempts were condemned because they threatened the parliamentary balance of power, for the electorate, unlike the King, was not part of the parliamentary balance at all : its function was to elect a constituent part of parliament but not to dictate to those it elected. The entry of the electorate into the constitution, greatly accelerated in 1832 but begun some fifty years before, came in the end to shatter a balance which has never been restored, for it thrust the King out of politics and gave both to the King's ministers and to the Commons a court of appeal, and indeed a master, outside parliament.

Because the Commons and the King's ministers were not, in practice, artificially bound together by the electorate, nor, in theory, bound together in any other way, the relationship of King and Commons dominated the whole of the period 1660–1832. The period began with an attempt to return, unconditionally, to the constitution as it was at the beginning of 1642, that is, to the old largely unwritten constitution as it had been modified by the early legislation of the Long Parliament. The attempt failed because it did not touch the problems which, in spite of this legislation, led to civil war and the abolition of kingship. The greatest of these problems was that of achieving co-operation between a king shorn of some of his prerogatives, and increasingly dependent financially on the Commons, and a House of Commons which, though aggressive and privileged, yet depended for its existence on the King. This problem was no nearer solution in 1660 than it was in 1642, and the next two reigns served only as a second commentary on the 1641 legislation. The uneasy co-operation of the first few years after the Restoration gave way, in the 1670s, to a series of charges by the Commons that the King was acting unconstitutionally, and before the end of Charles II's reign the Commons claimed, in the name of the constitution, the right to alter the succession and to prevent a Catholic from succeeding to the throne. The Commons failed to make good this claim only because their behaviour seemed, temporarily, to be more unconstitutional than the King's, and it was not long before James II, having succeeded to the throne in spite of his Catholicism, was opposed for his infringement of the constitution. The 1689 Revolution, by adding a good deal to the written constitution, reduced the size of the field within which it was possible for future kings to be unconstitutional. The reduction was taken further by the legislation of the next twenty-five years, which left no doubt that George I, a parliamentary king in a way in which William III had not been, was more and not less a king precisely because his title rested on parliamentary sanction and not on his own hereditary right. One of the ways in which parliament sought to confirm its right to make a king was by limiting the King's power to make a parliament, that is, to summon and dissolve one as he pleased. This was done, effectively and lastingly, by the Septennial Act of 1716, which marks the end of a period of constitutional definition. For although the Septennial Act did nothing more radical than to fix the maximum life of parliaments at seven years, in the following seventy years there was firmly established a constitutional idea that every parliament had a right to a life of seven years. Before 1716 fewer than half a dozen parliaments, since parliaments began, had lasted as long as seven years. Between 1716 and 1783 the 'Septennial convention' was regarded both by the King and by the Commons; between 1784 and 1832, though not always regarded by the King, it was still cherished by the Commons.

That parliament had a right to live for seven years was one of the two great conventions built in the eighteenth century upon the framework of legislation enacted in the period 1689–1716. It was a convention which increased the power of the House of Commons at the expense of the King, and it seemed not only to secure but also to symbolize the Commons' independence. The second great convention which was built upon the legislation of these years had the opposite effect: it weakened the Commons in relation to the King. At a time when, in the words of Thomas Hanmer, 'distrust of the executive

4

is the principle on which the whole of our Constitution is grounded', this second convention allowed a large number of members of parliament to be in some sense tied to the executive, that is, to hold office under the crown.

These two conventions were the main superstructure of the eighteenth-century constitution, for they provided and denoted a balance and a working relationship between King and Commons. Neither convention was free from attack. The first was attacked throughout the eighteenth century by those who wished to limit the power of the Commons, by reducing the period of seven years ; but it was not seriously challenged by the King until George III ignored it in 1784. The second was constantly attacked by those who wished to limit the power of the King, by excluding placemen from the House of Commons ; but it was not seriously undermined until, in the years between 1784 and the Reform Act, the administrative reforms of the younger Pitt and his successors drastically reduced the influence of the crown as an accidental corollary of increasing the efficiency of the executive government. The effect of these two conventions — the first weakening the King and the second weakening the Commons — was reinforced by the achievement of equilibrium between King and Commons in the sphere of finance. This financial equilibrium, again grounded upon legislation of the period 1689–1716, was also undermined before 1832.

If, then, the years from 1689 to 1716 are the formative years for the relation between King and Commons, the years from 1716 to 1783 are the years of balance between them, and in the years from 1784 to 1832 this balance was slowly undermined. Because the undermining was not simply the result of encroachment by the Commons on the King, as it might have been had it taken place at the end of the seventeenth century, the effect of the undermining was not simply to make the Commons at last victorious in a struggle which had been, for more than sixty years, suspended. Until 1867 the Commons enjoyed a period of qualified victory, but after 1867 it became apparent that the real victors were the electorate, and that King and Commons had exchanged their parliamentary partnership for a common subservience to an extra-parliamentary power.

CHAPTER II

THE SEPARATION OF KING
AND COMMONS, 1660–89

THE separation of King and Commons, within the framework of a parliamentary monarchy, was foreshadowed when the Commons first claimed that their privileges were not dependent on the King, when they tried to restrict the King's exercise of his prerogative of summoning and dissolving parliament at his discretion, and when they asserted that they were a permanent part of the constitution. These claims by the Commons to independence of the King were more radical than either parliament's abolition of the monarchy or the Commons' abolition of the House of Lords, for they modified the constitution while the abolition of the monarchy and the House of Lords only suspended it. The restoration of the House of Lords in February 1660 by the recalled Rump, and the decision that a parliament of two Houses should meet, without the King's command, took the separation further. The Commons' agreement with the Lords, on 1 May 1660, that 'according to the ancient and fundamental laws of this Kingdom, the Government is and ought to be, by King, Lords and Commons', called Charles II back to the throne of his father. But the statement did not embody a recantation. Rather it was a statement of achievement: it replaced the old unity of 'King in Parliament' by the new trinity of 'King, Lords and Commons', and the replacement was perhaps only unchallenged because it was clothed in a restoration.

The period between 1660 and 1689 showed how limited the achievement was. It became clear in these years that the separation of King and Commons could have little meaning, in practice, while the Commons still depended for their existence entirely on the King, and while the King was not obliged by financial needs to have a parliament always in existence. At the same time, the theoretical separation of King and Commons presented more openly the problem of their normal relationship, a problem only intermittently recognized before 1660 and ignored in 1660. In some sense, of course, the problem of co-operation between the King and a House of Commons elected at his command and for the purpose of doing him service had always existed, but it was not an acute problem so long as King and Commons were so unequally matched that the phrase 'King in Parliament' was an accurate description of their normal relationship. By 1660 this was no longer true. Yet the Restoration confirmed the separation of King and Commons without in any way providing for co-operation between them. Indeed, it seemed that the Restoration was an attempt to combine a new theory with an old practice. The attempt failed, and could hardly have had more than temporary success. The Revolution of 1689 confirmed the new theory, and the Revolution settlement began to make the old practice impossible by imposing serious restrictions on the King's prerogative in relation to parliament. These restrictions had little connection with the Restoration; they were essentially the complement of the restrictions imposed by the Long Parliament in 1641, and they, rather than the Restoration, mark the real end of an interregnum. Even so, the achievement of 1689 was still negative : legal restrictions placed on a King who remained head of the executive could at best serve as a basis for co-operation between King and Commons, and the methods of co-operation between them remained to be worked out. But at least it can be said that the restrictions were an adequate basis for co-operation, since, though they bound the King so tightly that he could not again hope to be sovereign, they did not exalt the Commons to a position of sovereignty.

The restoration of the King in 1660 was unconditional. Charles II was invited by the Convention Parliament to occupy the throne to which he had succeeded on his father's death in 1649. No new restrictions or limitations were placed upon him : the promises which he made at Breda in April 1660 — 'liberty to tender consciences', a 'free and general pardon' to all his subjects except those who might be named by parliament, willingness to assent to Acts of Parliament making these promises effective — were the expression of his personal wish for a moderate settlement and had no reference to his constitutional position and powers. Nor did the Convention Parliament refer to them except in its reply to the Declaration of Breda.

In intention this was a return to the constitutional position of 1642 and a renewal of the attempt, which had then failed, to establish constitutional monarchy by imposing certain statutory limitations on the King. The attempt was based, as it had been in 1642, on the legislation of the first ten months of the Long Parliament, which had been primarily designed to define as unconstitutional, in the narrower sense of unlawful, the means by which Charles I had been enabled to rule for eleven years without summoning a parliament. This legislation was not referred to in 1660. Its validity, however, was indirectly confirmed by an Act of 1661 declaring void all later ordinances and orders — which had not received the royal assent — and making it a treasonable offence to state that either or both Houses of Parliament had 'a Legislative Power without the King'. None of the 1641 legislation was modified until 1664. The Triennial Act was then repealed and replaced by a new one, stating that a new parliament should be summoned within three years of a dissolution, but leaving the King to summon it. It could be contended, therefore, that Charles II implicitly accepted certain limitations on his prerogative : that he could not tax his subjects without parliament's consent, that justice could be dispensed only in the common law courts and in the court of Chancery, that he had no means of enforcing his proclamations, which could implement but not make law, and that intervals of more than three years between parliaments were unlawful and, until 1664, liable to be ended by the election and meeting of a parliament without the King's order. But, beyond the implicit acceptance of the position which had in 1642 heralded civil war, and of the fact that the King's prerogative could be limited by statute, the Restoration settled nothing. If the Civil War had been fought because the 1641 settlement was inadequate, then the Restoration settlement, which could hardly be regarded as less inadequate, was not more likely to be successful. The period it inaugurated was indeed little more than an experiment to see whether a later generation could get on better in circumstances which their fathers had found impossible.

For the House of Commons these circumstances involved the abandonment of Cromwell's reform of the franchise and redistribution of seats and a return to its old composition and structure. Here, at least, restoration proved not incompatible with progress : the last step in the transfer from King to Commons of control over the membership of the House was taken in the 1670s, when the Commons challenged the King's power to create new parliamentary boroughs and to define the right of election in them.

The challenge had been foreshadowed in the early seventeenth century. Of the forty-one borough members added to the House of Commons between 1603 and 1660, only eleven were added by royal charter :[1] the rest were

---

[1] Three of the six charters purported to restore representation to boroughs (Harwich, Evesham, Bewdley) which had at some time sent members to parliament. The last charter, to Tiverton, was issued in 1615.

added not by statute but by Resolutions of the House of Commons. The Commons did not claim the right to create new constituencies. They resolved, however, on 4 May 1624, that 'a Borough cannot forfeit this Liberty of sending Burgesses, by *Non-user*', and, fortified by their acquisition of jurisdiction over disputed elections, they claimed that a Commons' Resolution was as competent as a royal charter to restore the privilege of representation to boroughs which could show that they had been represented in some former parliaments. Accordingly, eight boroughs were restored to representation by Commons' Resolutions in the 1620s, and seven were so restored during the Long Parliament. The Commons did not, after the Restoration, attempt to restore any boroughs to representation, but their attitude to the creation of a parliamentary borough at Newark by royal charter, in 1673, suggests that earlier restorations had in fact been associated with the claim, made openly in 1673, that the constitution of the House could only be altered by Act of parliament. Newark had no claim to be restored to representation, whether by King's charter or by Commons' Resolution. It had petitioned Elizabeth for representation in 1579 and been refused on the grounds that the House of Commons was large enough ; in 1644 Charles I had promised, but failed to grant, a new charter with an enfranchising clause. In 1661 Newark asked Charles II to honour his father's promise, and in March 1673 Charles II issued a charter giving Newark the right to send two burgesses to parliament, and stating that they should be elected by the mayor and aldermen. Two burgesses were so elected on 7 August 1673 ; the Commons refused to recognize the validity of the election and there followed three and a half years of petitioning by the two elected burgesses, their electors, and other inhabitants. The matter was complicated because the charter was found to contain several errors of fact and was returned to the King for amendment. None of the committees to which the petitions were referred seems to have come to a decision, and on 21 March 1677 the Commons heard the case at the bar of the House. It was argued, on the one hand, that the King had a right to restore boroughs to parliamentary representation by charter, but that new borough representation could only be created by Act of parliament; on the other, that the King had a right to create new borough representation by charter, but could not do so while parliament was sitting, for this opened the way to altering the complexion of an elected parliament; finally, that the King had a right to create new parliamentary boroughs at any time, whether or not parliament was sitting, but that he had no right to limit the franchise in those boroughs to a select body.[1] The last argument prevailed, and accordingly the Commons resolved that Newark had, by virtue of the royal charter, a right to send two burgesses to parliament, but resolved also that the men elected in 1673 were not duly elected. The Speaker was ordered to issue his warrant for a new writ and a new election was held on 19 April 1677.[2] In spite of his partial victory

[1] This argument, which had much to commend it, was not new: it had, for example, been expressed by Commons' Resolution in 1624 (John Glanville, *Reports of Certain Cases Determined and Adjudged by the Commons in Parliament in the Twenty-first and Twenty-second Years of the Reign of James I*, pp. 54-5 ; *Commons' Journals*, i. 759). The basis of the argument was that the borough franchise had originally corresponded to the county franchise, and should continue to do so when boroughs were 'taken out' of the counties for separate representation in parliament, and, further, that the right to send members to parliament was, for many boroughs, a prescriptive right, not dependent on incorporation. The definition of the franchise by charters of incorporation was, on this view, condemned as an unconstitutional infringement of rights. It should perhaps be added that the controversy in 1624 concerned a charter issued in 1553 to a borough, Chippenham, which had, intermittently, sent members to parliament before that date.

[2] One of the objections raised against the charter in the House of Commons, and incorporated in the Commons' second Resolution of March 1677, was its restriction of the electorate. The amended charter, which was issued in April 1677, after the Commons had ordered a new election, tacitly admitted the force of the Commons' complaint by providing for an electorate of mayor, aldermen, and all inhabitants paying scot and lot. The charter was surrendered to James II, who issued a new one in 1685 reserving

neither Charles nor any later monarch subsequently attempted to confer the right of representation by royal charter, though Shaftesbury's hope that the monarch's right to do so might be denied in law was never realized. The implications of the Commons' second Resolution were, however, not observed, and there is little doubt that, even in 1673, Charles's real interest was in the franchise rather than in the size of the House of Commons. The Commons, for their part, in spite of their acceptance, in 1677, of the King's right to enfranchise by charter, no longer wished the size of their House to be increased. They showed themselves unwilling to restore representation by Resolution,[1] and the enfranchisement of Durham in 1673, after the rejection of enfranchising Bills in 1660 and 1667, was the last statutory enfranchisement, apart from the Acts of Union with Scotland and Ireland, before 1832. Indeed, the only changes in the representation of England and Wales before 1832 were the statutory enlargement of the electorate of four boroughs (New Shoreham, 1770 ; Cricklade, 1782 ; Aylesbury, 1804 ; East Retford, 1828) and, in 1821, the statutory disfranchisement of Grampound and the transfer of its two members to Yorkshire. The fact that the number of representatives for England and Wales[2] remained at 513 between 1677 and 1832 was,

---

to the crown the right to remove all officials of the corporation. The general restoration of charters in October 1688 did not end controversy about the right of election in Newark : in January 1700 and again in March 1791 the Commons resolved, after controverted elections, that the right of election lay with mayor, aldermen, and inhabitants paying scot and lot (*Commons' Journals*, xiii. 111 ; xlvi. 335. T. H. B. Oldfield, *History of the Boroughs of Great Britain* (1792), ii. 368).

[1] In February 1694, Basingstoke, which had petitioned the Commons to be restored to representation, withdrew its petition 'by leave of the House' (*Commons' Journals*, xi. 85). This seems to have been the last petition for restoration of representation.

[2] Oldfield held the Act of Union with Scotland responsible for fixing the size of the House of Commons and so limiting the 'general right of the people to representation', for 'as the act of Union prescribed the number of members England and Scotland should send respectively to the parliament of Great Britain, it was an express condition of compact between the two nations, that no additional town or borough should be chartered to

then, not accidental, nor was it the reflection of a dead-lock between King and Commons : , it reflects, perhaps even more certainly than do the restorations of the first half of the seventeenth century, a deliberate policy on the part of the Commons.

The restoration of the franchise, in 1660, to its old form — uniform in the counties but very various in the boroughs, where it depended on custom or on the terms or interpretation of individual borough charters — was also incomplete. It too was undermined in part by statute and in part, and much more effectively, by the independent action of the King. The Corporation Act of 1661, which gave the King absolute control over the officers of the corporations for fifteen months, and a limited control thereafter, provided a basis for royal influence over elections. Charles II wished to extend the period of absolute control and, although he did not succeed in doing so, it is clear that, from the beginning of his reign, there existed a policy of influencing the composition of the Commons by restricting the borough franchise to borough officials, removable by the King.[1] The use of legal processes to effect the confiscation and remodelling of borough charters in the 1660s and 1670s more than counterbalanced the abeyance, after 1673, of the King's right to create new parliamentary boroughs by royal charter. After the dissolution of the Oxford parliament in March 1681 the royal policy became more systematic,

---

send members'. Thus the House of Commons had in a sense closed its own doors, and only the House of Commons could open them again. (*History of the Boroughs*, i. 109-12.) Although the Act of Union 'prescribed' Scotland's representation, it did not, except perhaps by implication, prescribe England's.

[1] Clarendon did not deny the charge made at his impeachment in 1667 'that he hath caused *Quo Warranto*'s to be issued against most of the corporations of *England*, immediately after their Charters were confirmed by Act of Parliament . . .' (*Commons' Journals*, ix. 16). But he maintained that 'he never caused any QUO WARRANTO to issue out against any one corporation in ENGLAND, but by his Majesty's express Command, or by Order of the Board ; which was always upon some miscarriage or Misbehaviour in the Corporation' (*Continuation of Life* (1759 ed.), pp. 949-50).

beginning with the proceedings against the corporation of London in December 1681, and had a more immediate object : the securing of a parliament which was not only favourable to the King but willing to support a particular royal policy. For Charles the policy was negative : his aim was to obtain a parliament firmly opposed to the policy of excluding James from the throne ; for James the policy was positive : he wished to obtain parliamentary sanction, based on an alliance between Catholics and Dissenters, for the repeal of the Test Acts and other penal ecclesiastical statutes. The measure of Charles's success was tested not during his own reign but in May 1685, at the first general election of James's reign. This election produced a parliament so favourably disposed towards James that, in Burnet's words, 'all men saw the way for packing a Parliament now open'. The measure of James's success was never fully tested : the parliament of 1685 proved to be not pliant enough to support his policy, and the effectiveness of his own confiscation and modification of charters, and his widespread dismissals of borough officers, could only have been tested by the summons of a second parliament. The attack on the corporations, then, could claim no clear success in the shape of policy, but it had a marked effect both on the eighteenth-century borough franchise and on eighteenth-century borough government. For the very fact that the policy of remodelling endured for more than twenty-five years established vested interests which were often impossible to uproot. Many boroughs kept their restricted franchise : in spite of James's proclamation of 4 October 1688, restoring London's charters, and his proclamation of 17 October, restoring all forfeited charters and discharging all borough officers put in since 1679, and in spite of the restoration of a few charters in William III's reign,[1] the

---

[1] In the spring of 1689 and in December Bills were introduced into the House of Commons providing for a general restoration of Charters — both

most conspicuous legacy of the remodelling policy is seen in the numerous disputes, inside and outside parliament, about the right of election in boroughs. In judging these disputes, which continued throughout the eighteenth century, the House of Commons did not often side with the advocates of a wide franchise.

The place of the House of Commons in the constitution depends, in the last resort, less on its composition and the manner of its election than on how often parliaments are summoned and how long parliaments last. Here the Restoration seemed more complete. Since the sixteenth century, when service in parliament began to be regarded as a privilege instead of as a burden, there had been many requests for frequent parliaments, often supported by an appeal to 'the statutes made in the reign of Edward III', that is, statutes of 1330 and 1362 which, in the words of the Triennial Act of 1641, required that 'The parliament ought to be holden at least once every year for the redress of grievances'.[1] The promoters of the Triennial Act of 1641 did not suppose that these statutes provided for the summoning of a new parliament every year, nor did they regard this as desirable. For, after declaring that the statutes of Edward III should in future be observed, the Triennial Act established machinery to ensure that not more than three years should elapse between the dissolving or proroguing of one parliament and the summoning of the next. The Act was repealed, on the grounds that it was destructive of the King's just rights and prerogative, by an Act of 1664. The new Act

seem to have been frustrated by prorogation. In the debate on the second Bill the chief point at issue was whether the surrenders had been legal: the Commons' decision, in January 1690, that 'Charters may be surrendered as occasion serves' was followed in March by the introduction of a Bill to restore the privileges of the City of London. This became law, but there were no more Bills dealing with corporations as a whole.

[1] The phrase in the 1330 statute is 'que parlement soit tenu chescun an, une foitz, ou plus si mestier soit', and in the 1362 statute, 'soit parlement tenuz chescun an' (*Statutes of the Realm*, i. 265, 374).

confined itself to exhortation, declaring that, in accordance with the laws of Edward III which required parliaments to be held very often, there should not elapse more than three years between the dissolution of one parliament and the issue of writs for another 'to the end that there may be a frequent calling, assembling and holding of Parliaments once in three years at the least'. The provision against long prorogations was not repeated. There is evidence that the Triennial Act of 1664 was thought to be ineffective. In February 1668, for example, Sir Richard Temple, member for Buckingham, introduced a Bill which aimed to secure 'the frequent holding of parliaments' by reviving the machinery of the 1641 Act.[1] The Bill was read a first time but was then withdrawn on the technical ground that it had been introduced without leave, and the proposal seems to have been dropped. In December 1680 a Commons' Resolution in favour of the introduction of a Bill for frequent parliaments was frustrated by dissolution. Nevertheless, whether or not the 1664 Act was effective, its intention was certainly fulfilled in the general sense that, in the next thirty years, the longest interval between parliaments was the period of four years between the dissolution of the last parliament of Charles II in March 1681 and the meeting of the first parliament of James II in May 1685. Moreover, none of the intervals between Charles II's five parliaments was longer than a few months.[2] Again,

[1] It is significant that Temple pressed for triennial parliaments, and did not hesitate to declare that annual parliaments, required by the statutes of Edward III, were 'too frequent, and therefore laid aside'. In this he showed more historical sense than later advocates of annual general elections, whose legalistic stand upon the statutes of Edward III in effect threatened all the advance made by parliament since the fourteenth century. The fourteenth-century meaning of the phrase 'parlement soit tenu' could only be applied at the end of the seventeenth century if the clock were put back. Indeed, drafters of the Triennial Acts of 1641, 1664, and 1694 implicitly admitted this by citing the fourteenth-century statutes as justification for triennial parliaments.

[2] Compare the intervals of Elizabeth's reign and James I's reign : five of the intervals between Elizabeth's ten parliaments lasted between three and five years ; the intervals between James's four parliaments were three years, six and a half years, two years.

in the thirty years after 1664 no prorogation lasted as long as two years, and Charles II's long parliament had sixteen sessions.[1] These facts are not less startling because they can be ascribed rather to the increased practical difficulties of living without parliament than to the Triennial Act of 1641, which can hardly have been said to have been tested, or to the 1664 Act.

On the other other hand, the duration of parliaments varied as much in Charles II's reign as it had done in Elizabeth's, and from this point of view parliament seemed no less a creature of the King after the Restoration than it had been before the accession of the Stuarts. All the parliaments summoned by Charles II, except the Cavalier Parliament, were very short, and James II's only parliament, which met in May 1685, was prorogued in November and dissolved, after five more prorogations, in July 1687. This record is not very different from that of Elizabeth and the early Stuarts : except for Elizabeth's second parliament, 1562–6, and her long third one, 1572–83, all her parliaments were short, usually lasting only two or three months ; of James I's parliaments, the first one was long, 1603–10, and the other three short; none of Charles I's parliaments, except the Long Parliament, lasted for more than a year. The duration of parliament, as distinct from the frequency of parliamentary sessions, depends directly on the King's prerogative of dissolution, and any tampering with this prerogative is clearly more radical than attempts to secure regular meetings of parliament. The only legislation which touched this prerogative before 1660 was the Triennial Act of 1641, which tried to secure a minimum life for parliament by requiring the King not to dissolve or prorogue any parliament, without its own consent, within fifty days of its first meeting. This curtailment of the prerogative of dissolution was removed by the new Triennial Act of 1664, and, indeed, the Com-

[1] Compare the three sessions of Elizabeth's long parliament of 1572–83.

mons slowly began to see that their interests now lay rather in curtailing the prerogative in the opposite direction, and pressing rather for a maximum than for a minimum life for parliament.

The idea that it was desirable to limit the life of a parliament was put forward, tentatively and unsuccessfully, during the parliament of 1661–79, which lasted longer than a parliament had ever lasted before, and met for some part of every year of its existence except 1672 and 1676. In October 1675 the Commons discussed a proposal made by Sir Harbottle Grimstone, a former Speaker, that the King should be asked 'to put a period to this parliament. . . . There is a great mischief in the length of this parliament, as if there were no parliament. A Standing Parliament is as inconvenient as a Standing Army'. The proposal seems to have been dropped, but in November a motion in the Lords for an address to the King, praying him not to prorogue but to dissolve parliament, was only lost by 48 votes to 50. The motion was strongly pressed by Shaftesbury, and his arguments were repeated in the Protest, signed by twenty-two peers, against the rejection of the motion. These peers asserted that 'frequent and new parliaments' were part of the constitution and that 'the practice of several hundred years hath been accordingly'; that the existing House of Commons was no longer representative of the electorate; that long parliaments fostered parties and factions, for example the recent 'unhappy Breach fallen out between the two houses' over Dr. Shirley's case. Immediately after the Protest was made parliament was prorogued until February 1677. When it met again the Duke of Buckingham, supported by Shaftesbury, Salisbury, and Wharton, contended in the House of Lords that parliament had been automatically dissolved by reason of its prorogation, for a period of fifteen months, in contravention of the statutes of Edward III which required it to meet every year. He therefore moved that the King be asked 'to give us speedily a new Parliament'. The House thought Buckingham's speech 'bold and shocking' and committed him and his supporters to the Tower. In the House of Commons Sir John Mallett made a more moderate proposal : he did not deny that the parliament still legally existed, since the King had not dissolved it, but he questioned the legality of the prorogation, and proposed an address to the King "that he will be pleased to dissolve this, and very quickly call another parliament'. Although the proposal had some support, it was disliked both by those who resented any attempt to influence the King's use of his prerogative and by those who resented the interference of the Lords in a question; dissolution, which was considered to be primarily the concern of the Commons. The contention that a prorogation of more than a year was tantamount to a dissolution was put forward also outside parliament, notably in the pamphlet *Whether a Prorogation of the Parliament, extended beyond Twelve months, be not, in construction of law, dissolution?* The author maintained that the statutes of Edward III made prorogations of more than a year illegal, and, therefore, that a prorogued parliament ceased to be a legal one, and was dissolved, at the moment when its prorogation ceased to be legal. The wider issue, that of long parliaments, was also argued outside parliament. The author of the *Inconveniences of a long Continuance of the same Parliament*, published in 1680, escaped the charge of attacking the King's prerogative by pleading that long parliaments were not an advantage but a disadvantage to the King, and that 'not only the proroguing, but the frequent dissolving of parliaments, is absolutely necessary for the preservation of monarchy'. Long parliaments, he insisted, were 'the most pernicious thing imaginable both to king and people', and benefited only their members, who 'having long beheld the tempting, though forbidden fruit of

supremacy, [they] have not scrupled to grapple with the
king, for a share of the sovereignty'. These arguments,
although perhaps designed to appeal to the King, were
not those usually advanced against long parliaments.
More common were the arguments put forward in 1668
and 1675, that long parliaments were illegal, and that they
were, like standing armies, steps towards tyranny ; and
behind these arguments lay the feeling, not always openly
expressed until after 1689, that a long parliament was
ipso facto congenial to the King who chose to keep it in
existence, and that it was congenial to him because he had
found ways of securing its subservience.[1] There seemed,
therefore, good reason to expect that, if the Commons
again restricted the King's prerogative by legislation, they
would try to limit the life of parliaments as well as the
length of the intervals between parliaments, and they did
so immediately after 1689. Before 1689, however, there
were no more long parliaments, and no more attempts to
restrict the King's freedom to dissolve or retain parliaments
at his will.

Yet the relations of Charles and James with their
parliaments show that, between 1660 and 1689, the King's
unfettered power of dissolution was not an adequate
answer to the problem of his relationship with the Commons, and they show on the King's part some awareness
of this fact. The modification of borough charters, an
attempt to make the relationship smoother by making the
electorate more conservative, proved to have a very limited
effect on the kind of men returned to the Commons. Far

[1] Sir John St. Aubyn's description, in 1734, of Charles II's long parliament, is typical of the views of the advocates of short parliaments.
Charles II, he said, 'took a surfeit of Parliaments in his father's time, and
was therefore extremely desirous to lay them aside : but this was a scheme
impracticable. However, in effect he did so : for he obtained a Parliament,
which by its long duration, like an Army of Veterans, became so exactly
disciplined to his own measures, that they knew no other command but
from that person who gave them their pay. This was a safe and most
ingenious way of enslaving a nation' (*Parliamentary History*, ix. 401).

more important were approaches made during the long parliament of 1661–79 towards the organization of the King's supporters within the House of Commons into a court party, cemented by the distribution to them of crown offices, pensions, and other favours belonging to crown patronage. These approaches had, as a corollary, attempts to organize critics of the King and his ministers into a country party, independent of royal favours and therefore more difficult to hold together except in times of crisis. The court and country parties, which in this period were at their most successful under the leadership of Danby and Shaftesbury, were then labelled Tory and Whig. The labels change their meaning after 1689, after 1714, and again after 1760, but the change cannot diminish the importance of a division, based on support of or opposition to the court, which lasted until the middle of the nineteenth century, nor the fact that the division, even at its most rigid, never included the whole House.

To contemporaries the building up of a court party in the House of Commons was evidence of an attempt to undermine the independence of its members, and the building up of an opposition party was, on the same grounds, only less pernicious. There was, therefore, in and after the 1670s, much talk of parliamentary corruption. None of the proposals for checking it had any success before 1689, but they were all in some measure incorporated in statute in the period between the Revolution and the coming of the Hanoverians, and they formed the prototype of all eighteenth-century attempts to safeguard the independence of the Commons from the King's influence. The old wish for frequent parliaments came to include a new wish that parliaments should be short, on the grounds that parliaments which lasted only one year, or only three years, would be less easily corrupted than long or unlimited parliaments. The Declaration of Rights repeated the old assertion that parliaments ought to be held frequently, but no statutory limitation on the life of a parliament was prescribed until the Triennial Act of 1694. More progress was made with the proposal to strengthen the Commons against crown influence by forbidding members of parliament to hold crown offices or pensions. The first Place Bill, introduced into the House of Commons on 29 April 1675, provided that members who accepted office should lose their seats but should be allowed to stand for election again, either at the ensuing by-election or later. The Bill was defeated by 145 votes to 113 on the motion to send it to committee. On 30 December 1680 the House of Commons resolved that its members should ask the permission of the House before accepting office, and that any member who did not do so should be expelled. A combination of unpropitious circumstances — the dissolution of parliament in January 1681, the one-week parliament of March 1681, and the absence of parliament for the rest of Charles's reign, followed by the short sitting of James's only parliament — meant that the Resolution was not observed and the penalty not exacted. The Declaration of Rights, concerned primarily with the King's prerogative rather than with his influence, did not mention placemen. In the 1690s, however, a series of Place Bills were introduced into the Commons, and in the eighteenth century Place Bills became a recognized method of expressing discontent with the government. A demand complementary to the exclusion of placemen, that members of parliament should be elected freely, was included in the Declaration of Rights and also formed the subject of statutes in the 1690s and in the early eighteenth century.

Charles II's Cavalier Parliament, then, showed the Commons the dangers of a long parliament and stimulated plans, which were adopted in and after 1689, for checking the King's influence over the Commons. On the other hand, the last six years of his reign, and the whole reign of James II, showed that the more fundamental dangers of dissolution and absence of parliament had not passed. These years recalled the Commons from a seemingly premature concern with influence to their earlier concern with prerogative. It is true that these years also showed that the King's success in reducing the Commons to servility had not yet been very great, but this was of secondary importance, for it seemed that the King could still dispense with parliament for a period longer than that stipulated in the 1664 Triennial Act, and, by doing so, could in the last resort force his policy against the Commons.

Charles was helped in this because, although some of his actions before 1679 had been criticized as unconstitutional, after 1679 his policy seemed to be conservative, while the policy of his opponents in the Commons, who were in a majority despite tampering with the borough franchise and pressure at elections, seemed radical. Indeed, the Commons' policy, to alter the succession on the grounds that the heir to the throne was a Catholic, was an attempt to extend from subjects to monarch the principle of the Test Acts, which had followed the Commons' successful opposition to Charles's Declaration of Indulgence in 1672. The Test Acts prevented Catholics from holding office under the crown and from sitting in parliament; the three Exclusion Bills, introduced into the House of Commons in 1679, 1680, and 1681, would have prevented the Catholic heir from holding the crown itself. In face of the first Bill, which seemed likely to pass the Commons, Charles first prorogued and then dissolved parliament; in face of the second, which passed the Commons but was rejected in the Lords, he again dissolved parliament; in face of the third he immediately dissolved parliament, and for the rest of his reign, in defiance of the Triennial Act of 1664, ruled without one.

Thus there was no other tangible reason for the failure

of the attempt to exclude James from the throne than that
Charles's use of the prerogative of dissolution was not
countered in the only way in which it could have been
effectively countered — by the imposition of something
like the limitations imposed on Charles I after 1642. On
the contrary, in face of the extravagant threats of the
Exclusionists, and open talk of civil war, constitutional
issues were submerged beneath emotional ones : on the
one hand, fear of civil war and of anarchy, and on the other,
the feeling that divine right kingship was a safeguard
against these evils. In spite of his dissolutions of parliament in the cause of hereditary monarchy, Charles's conduct seemed not immoderate, and could even be represented
as designed to protect the Church of England : in April
1679 he offered to agree to the placing of limitations on a
Catholic successor, and in March 1681 he offered to assent
to a Bill which should ensure that the 'administration of
government' after his death should 'remain in Protestant
hands'. It is perhaps not surprising that the absence of
parliament for four years did not prevent James from
succeeding on a wave of royalist feeling. James, for his
part, was moved to promise that he would protect the
Church of England. But he was justified in not regarding
this promise as a condition of his accession, and he had at
least reasonable justification for his belief that neither
Anglicans nor Tories would, in any circumstances, resist
a king. Nevertheless, constitutional issues only remained
submerged for the short period during which James seemed
to have no other drawbacks than his popery. The Commons' Resolution of 29 January 1689, to which the Lords
agreed, that it was 'inconsistent with the welfare of this
Protestant Kingdom to be ruled by a Popish prince', the
unqualified exclusion of Catholics from the throne in
the Declaration of Rights, and finally the statement in the
Act of Settlement that the King should take an oath to
uphold the Church of England 'as by law established',

C

not only vindicated the Exclusionists' policy but finally transferred from King to parliament the ordering of the relation between the King and the established church.

The problem of dissolution remained, and could not be solved by legislation excluding certain kinds of king from the throne. Charles had used dissolution as a negative weapon : he had prorogued and dissolved parliaments and ruled without parliament in order to prevent the Commons from effecting a policy distasteful to him. James used dissolution as a positive weapon : he prorogued and finally dissolved parliament in order to prevent the Commons from criticizing a policy distasteful to them. His policy was fundamentally distasteful on religious grounds, but his methods of carrying it out were more than distasteful : they drew attention not only to the fact that the prerogative of dissolution was unfettered, but also to the inadequacies of the 1641 settlement as regards the supremacy of statute law. Charles's suspension of the ecclesiastical penal laws in 1672 was withdrawn when the Commons, supported by the Lords, protested the illegality of suspension except by Act of parliament. But parliament was prorogued in November 1685 when the Commons protested against James's dispensations from those laws, and no parliamentary protest was therefore possible against his later suspension of them. Moreover, some of the judges upheld James's right to dispense not only from ecclesiastical laws but from all laws, and this made nonsense of parliament's legislative supremacy.

It was no wonder then that the Revolution settlement repaired the inadequacies of the 1641 settlement by depriving the King of this channel of independent legislative power. The Bill of Rights declared unlawful for the future the use of both the dispensing power (unless specifically authorized in the statute dispensed from) and the suspending power. The King was never deprived by statute of his right of refusing his assent to Bills passed by both Houses, but the practice of refusal had become infrequent even before 1660. Charles only refused the royal assent twice, in 1662 and 1678, and James never did so. William refused his assent five times, notably to three Bills designed to restrict the royal prerogative — in 1692 to a Bill providing that judges should hold office during good behaviour, in February 1693 to a Triennial Bill, in January 1694 to a Place Bill. His refusal to assent to the Place Bill, 'An Act touching free and impartial proceedings in Parliament', provoked the Commons to remind him that his predecessors had rarely refused their assent to Bills passed by both Houses, and that 'the few instances in former reigns where such assent hath not been given' had been 'attended with great inconveniences to the Crown of England, especially where the same hath been withheld by insinuations of particular persons, without the advice of the Privy Council, thereby creating great dissatisfaction and jealousies in the minds of your people'. Anne's single refusal, in 1708, went unchallenged by the Commons, and is remarkable only because it was the last. As far as legislation went, parliament seemed to have vindicated its supremacy and, in this sphere, not only to have deprived the King of independent power but also to have deprived him, in practice, of his position of equality with the other two parts of parliament.

In other ways, too, the 1689 settlement completed that of 1641 by adding to the explicit restrictions then placed on the King's prerogative. It touched the King's executive powers by confirming that extra-parliamentary taxation was unlawful, and by providing that the raising or maintenance of a standing army in time of peace, as James had maintained one after the suppression of Monmouth's rebellion, was unlawful without the consent of parliament. On the other hand, the settlement placed no direct restriction on the King's position as head of the executive, and indeed it confirmed, if only by silence, the King's power to choose his servants freely. In this it showed, like the 1641 settlement but unlike the Grand Remonstrance, a willingness that, in his own sphere, the King should be independent and separate from parliament.

There is, however, one vital difference between 1689 and 1641 which is not merely one of degree : the legislation of 1641 curtailed the prerogative of an existing monarch, whose title to the throne did not depend on parliament or on his acceptance of parliament's limitations ; the Declaration of 1689 curtailed the prerogative of a future monarch, whose title to the throne depended on parliament and whose place on the throne was conditional on his acceptance of parliament's limitations. Similar limitations might have been imposed on the Stuarts in 1660 or in 1679 : the fact that they were not is a sign that it was easier to bind a monarch created by parliament than a monarch restored by parliament, and this is perhaps the only reason why the King came to owe his existence to parliament as parliament had always owed its existence to the King.

For this was the safeguard of the 1689 settlement : that William and Mary succeeded to the throne only after and because they accepted the limitations it imposed. The greater problem was that of justifying their title to the throne. The logical justification would have been that parliament had deposed James because he refused to accept the limitations which, explicitly placed on William and Mary, had yet implicitly bound James. The Commons' Resolution of 28 January 1689, which preceded the drawing up of the Declaration of Rights, went only half way towards this theory of kingship : it stated that James had 'endeavoured to subvert the constitution of this kingdom by breaking the original contract between King and People', and that he had 'violated the fundamental laws'. But the 'vacancy' of the throne was explained not as the result of James's breach of contract and violation of the fundamental laws but as the result of his abdication — itself a fiction which the Lords were only with difficulty persuaded to accept. Finally, the Resolution did not explain why William and Mary should fill the vacancy. The Resolution was, of course, a compromise designed to antagonize as few as possible of the opponents of James's government. James had certainly set aside statute law, but to say that this was reason for Lords and Commons to depose him seemed near to asserting not only parliament's legislative supremacy but parliament's sovereignty, and, indeed, the sovereignty of Lords and Commons. Many supporters of the Revolution, including Locke, were unwilling to admit even parliament's sovereignty, which they distinguished from parliament's supremacy in the legislative sphere, and they tended therefore to justify the Revolution on the grounds that James had broken the 'fundamental laws' which bound both King and Parliament but emanated from neither. Others, like James Tyrrell in *Bibliotheca Politica*, delved into the past to prove that in England a contract between King and People was a historical fact, for a contract had formed the basis of the elective Anglo-Saxon monarchy, and this contract, though temporarily abrogated by the Norman Conquest, had been restored by later charters and 'treaties' between King and subjects. The idea of a contract, whether historical or merely implicit, certainly seems to provide a better theoretical basis for mixed monarchy than the idea of fundamental laws. For the nature of the fundamental laws must depend in the last resort on personal interpretation, and opponents as well as supporters of the Revolution appealed for justification to the 'fundamental laws', which they tended to equate with the laws of nature or the laws of God. The contention put forward in *A brief Account of the Nullity of King James' Title*, that the 'particular' fundamental laws of England require 'that the whole legislative power should not be lodged in the hands of the King alone' is, after all, not easy to prove without reference to laws made by parliament.

Moreover, there was an evident tendency after 1689 to regard the Declaration of Rights, which was in fact enacted as a statute, as a fundamental law, and this, while perhaps making the conception of fundamental law clearer, diminishes the force of the contention that fundamental law is something greater than statute law and cannot be changed by statute law. The Declaration of Rights, presented to and accepted by William and Mary on 13 February, made no reference either to fundamental laws or to a contract between King and People : its charge against James was simply that he had 'endeavoured to extirpate the Protestant religion and the lawes and Liberties of this Kingdom'.[1] The enactment of the Declaration of Rights on 16 December was the statutory institution of conditional kingship for the future. The coronation oath, modified accordingly, bound the King to maintain, instead of the laws and customs granted by previous Kings, the 'statutes in Parliament agreed upon' and 'the Protestant reformed religion established by law'. This was a lasting modification. But the matching amendment of the oath of allegiance, which deprived William and Mary of the description 'rightful and lawful' enjoyed by their predecessors, was only temporary. The restoration of these words in 1696, by the Act sanctioning the oath of the Association to defend William, and the addition in 1701 of a new oath, declaring that the Pretender 'hath not any right or title whatsoever to the crown of this realm', sealed the deposition of one king and his supersession by another who was no less a king.

[1] Cf. Bishop Stillingfleet : 'If once we depart from the ancient and legal constitution of Parliaments, there will be no end of alterations.—Every new modeller of government hath something to offer that looks like reason, at least to those whose interest it is to carry it on : and, if no precedents can be found, then they appeal to a certain invisible theory called *The Fundamental Contract of the Nation*, which, being nowhere to be found, may signify what anyone pleases.' (*Works* (1707-10), iii. 874).

The experience of the 1670s had shown the difficulties of dealing with problems of influence while the problem of prerogative was still unsolved, and the settlement of 1689 made little attempt to do so. Nevertheless, in a very few of its provisions the 1689 settlement looked not only backwards, to the problem of the limitation of the King's prerogative, but also forwards, to the problem of the relations between King and Commons and the safeguarding of the independence of the House of Commons by limiting the King's influence over it. There is in the Declaration of Rights no reference either to placemen or to the duration of parliaments ; the questions of the frequency of parliaments and the freedom of elections are mentioned, though they are dealt with only by injunction. But even this very tentative approach was a small step towards the recognition that limitation of the King's prerogative was only a negative achievement. It could provide a basis for the working of parliamentary monarchy, but it could not ensure a normal working relationship between King and Commons. So, while the settlement as a whole foreshadows the further, and final, statutory limitations placed by the Act of Settlement on a king who did not, as William and Mary did, succeed one who had broken the contract between King and subjects, a few clauses of the Declaration faintly foreshadow the approaches made in the period 1689–1716 to the problem of the relationship between a limited King and a strong but not sovereign House of Commons.

CHAPTER III

THE FRAMEWORK OF EIGHTEENTH-CENTURY GOVERNMENT

(i) THE LIFE OF THE COMMONS

THE framework of eighteenth-century government, erected in the main by legislation enacted in the years between 1689 and 1716, provided a qualified independence for the Commons. This was a compromise. It arrested the advance of the Commons' powers no less than the decline of the King's, and it made possible, and in a sense fostered, the growth of connections between King and Commons which kept the balance of the constitution after 1716. The first element in the framework, the life of the Commons, cut directly across the King's fundamental prerogative in relation to parliament, his right of summoning and dissolving it at will. For Parliament was the creature of the King: attendance in parliament, which had been a feudal obligation, remained a duty owed to the King, and the length of time for which parliaments lasted was a matter for the King alone. Indeed, since 'the King is indisputably invested with the right of assembling parliaments', de Lolme, in 1775, maintained that laws made 'to restrain the use of' this right were not ordinary laws but 'express and solemn conventions . . . or treaties with the Body of the People'. The Commons attempted to make such treaties very early in the history of parliament. The plea that parliaments should be held 'very often', first uttered at a time when parliaments sat for a few weeks and did little, echoed anachronistically in the sixteenth and seventeenth centuries, when parliaments lasted longer and did more. In the sixteenth century, especially during those parliaments which lasted for several years, the plea for frequent parliaments was accompanied by complaints of numerous prorogations and short sessions, and in the seventeenth century the plea was accompanied by complaints that parliaments were dissolved too soon after their first meeting and that the intervals between parliaments were too long. Nevertheless, in spite of these tentative approaches to the problem of how long a parliament should last, the main plea was still that parliaments should be held frequently: that they should be not extraordinary and occasional events but a regular part of the constitution. Even the Triennial Act of 1641 had as its prime object the prevention of the 'Inconveniencies happening by the long Intermission of Parliaments', and was not bold enough to do more about the question of duration than to prescribe a small minimum life of fifty days. The more radical Act of the same year, which provided that the then parliament should not be dissolved or prorogued without its own consent — an indefinite suspension of the King's prerogative in relation to the parliament which passed the Act — was carefully phrased as an emergency measure. The maximum period of three years between parliaments, prescribed by the Triennial Act of 1641 and repeated both by the Triennial Act of 1664 and the Triennial Act of 1694, proved to be the final statutory solution of the problem of the intervals between parliaments. Indeed, the Triennial Act of 1664 was not repealed until 1887, and even then it was repealed only on the ground that the 1694 Act rendered it unnecessary.[1]

[1] The statutes of 1330 and 1362 were repealed, as obsolete, in 1881 and 1863 respectively. Clearly they had had no practical effect since the time in which they were appropriate, the fourteenth and fifteenth centuries, though it may reasonably be argued that their requirement was, in spirit, met by the annual sessions of the period after 1689. The advocates of annual parliaments after 1689 did not, of course, admit this, and continued to appeal to the letter of the laws.

33

In fact, however, intervals of as long as three years were already impossible even in 1694, and practical necessity, in the shape of financial stringency, had already introduced the system under which a new parliament is summoned when the old one is dissolved. The same practical necessity made annual meetings of parliament unavoidable, though they have never been prescribed by statute: the only attempt to prescribe them, in the first Triennial Bill of January 1693, was the main cause of William III's refusal of assent to the Bill.

The idea that it was also desirable to prescribe a maximum life for parliament was a later one. It was stimulated by Charles II's Cavalier Parliament, but not strongly or consistently advocated until after 1689. The statutory achievement of a reasonably long maximum parliamentary life in 1716 proved, moreover, far more valuable than its advocates realized, for it gave rise to the further idea that every parliament should last for the same length of time, and that parliament's statutory maximum life was, in fact, the normal and natural life to which each parliament was entitled. This idea became a firm convention though it was never translated into statute. It was of vital importance, for it made parliament not wholly the King's creature, and completed the transition, begun in 1641, from 'King in parliament' to 'King, Lords, and Commons'. This transition, and indeed the prerogative of dissolution in general, was held by the Commons to be their particular concern rather than the concern of Lords and Commons jointly. For the Lords, in de Lolme's words, 'enjoyed a dignity which is hereditary, as well as inherent to their persons, and form a permanent Body in the State; whereas the Commons completely vanish, whenever a dissolution takes place'. The life of parliament, then, was only truly a matter of life and death for the Commons.

The achievement of a regular life, like the achievement of annual meetings of parliament and the ending of long intervals between parliaments, was in part accidental, and, though the Commons gained more from it than the Lords, it was certainly not secured, in the event, by the Commons' unilateral action. It seemed, indeed, that it would be more difficult to secure a regular and limited life for parliament than to secure annual sessions or to end long intervals between parliaments. On the one hand, limitation of parliament's life appeared to be a more flagrant invasion of the King's prerogative, since the power to dissolve at will was more fundamental than the power to summon at will. On the other hand, there was clearly no way of effecting the limitation except by statute, and many advocates of limitation made their task more difficult by trying to include in the limiting statute not only provision for annual sessions but also machinery to ensure that the statute was not evaded. In December 1689, for example, a Bill was introduced to repeal the Triennial Act of 1664, and revive the 1641 machinery to secure the summoning of a parliament, after an interval of three years, without the King's warrant. This Bill provided also that no parliament should last for more than three years or be dissolved in less than fifty days, and that there should be annual sessions. The Bill was frustrated first by the prorogation and then by the dissolution of parliament. Again, in February 1693, William refused his assent to a Bill providing for new parliaments every three years, the holding of parliament every year, and the determination of the existing parliament in March 1694.[1] The Commons themselves rejected, in November and December of the same year, two

---

[1] The Bill, introduced into the House of Lords by Shrewsbury after the defeat of the 1692 Place Bill, originally provided for annual general elections as well as annual sessions. As passed by the Lords it provided for general elections every three years, annual sessions, and the determination of the existing parliament in January 1694. Although the Commons passed the Bill, by 200 to 161, only altering the date of determination to March 1694, they clearly showed resentment that the Lords should have taken the initiative in regulating parliament's life — a matter primarily for the Commons.

Bills providing for new parliaments every three years. It seems that the Commons acted in this way mainly because the first Bill, which originated in the Commons, did not provide for annual sessions, and because the second Bill was introduced and sent down from the Lords. The Triennial Act of 1694, which was also introduced in the House of Lords, was a compromise. It dealt again with the old problems, already dealt with in 1641 and 1664, of frequent parliaments and intervals between parliaments, and it dealt with the new problem of the life of parliament, but it contained no provision for annual sessions, and it established no machinery of enforcement. To the old assertion that 'by the ancient Laws and Statutes of this Kingdom frequent Parliaments ought to be held', the Act of 1694 added the new assertion that 'frequent and new Parliaments tend very much to the happy union and good agreement of King and People'. Accordingly, the Act stated that the life of every future parliament should be limited to three years and that the existing parliament, which had met in March 1690, must be dissolved on 1 November 1696 unless the King and Queen dissolved it sooner. An unsuccessful attempt was made, in the House of Lords, to alter the date of determination to 1 November 1695;[1] in fact William did not wait for parliament to determine but used his prerogative and dissolved it in October 1695. In 1696, after the Assassination Plot, parliament's life was further separated from the King by an Act which provided that the monarch's death should not automatically dissolve parliament, but that either the existing parliament, or, if none existed, its predecessor, should meet and continue in existence for six months

[1] November 1695 was the original date. It was altered to November 1696 in the Commons and reached the Lords in this form. Four peers, Halifax, Devonshire, Aylesbury, and Weymouth, entered a protest against the later date 'because it tendeth to the Continuance of this present Parliament longer than, as we apprehend, is agreeable with the Constitution of England' (H. C. Foxcroft, *Life and Letters of Sir George Savile, first Marquis of Halifax*, ii. 184).

unless the new monarch dissolved it sooner. This provision was repeated in 1705, and in 1707 after the Union
with Scotland, and, with a modification in 1797 to cover
the case of a monarch who died in the interval between the
summons and the meeting of a parliament, it lasted until
1867, when the second Reform Act provided that the death
of a monarch should have no effect on the life of the then
parliament.

The first parliament summoned by William and Mary
lasted for five and a half years, from March 1690 to October
1695. Seven of the nine parliaments summoned between
1695 and 1714 lasted between two and three years, two
lasted for less than a year. Even the longest of these nine
parliaments, that of June 1705 to April 1708 and that of
November 1710 to August 1713, did not last long enough
for any kind of organization or smooth working, and this
did not further the Commons' independence. Party dis-
sensions and confusions increased, and corruption and
manipulation were intensified : the frequent debates in
the House of Commons about bribery, intervention at
elections, and influence of all kinds during the twenty
years of the operation of the Triennial Act leave no doubt
about this. At least these years proved that a series of
short parliaments, with short intervals between them, did
not make for stability, and they suggested also that the
holding of frequent general elections, so that 'the heats
and animosities raised on such occasions had no time to
subside', weakened instead of strengthening the Commons.
In 1716, by the Septennial Act, the period within which
a parliament must be dissolved was increased to seven
years. The Septennial Act proved to be one of the most
important factors in the stability of eighteenth-century
government, for it gave parliament a normal, regular, and
reasonably long life of its own, and so immensely reduced
its dependence on the King. This result was not implicit
in the Act, which stated, not that every parliament should

last for seven years, but that none should last for more than seven, as, of course, the Triennial Act had stated that no parliament should last for more than three years.   None the less, the Septennial Act came to be interpreted (as the Triennial Act had not been) as if it prescribed not the maximum but the normal life of a parliament : the King was content to allow his prerogative of earlier dissolution to fall into abeyance, and the Commons behaved as if he did not possess it.   Every parliament summoned between 1716 and 1783, except that dissolved by George I's death in 1727, lasted for more than five and a half years ; all but two lasted for more than six years.   These two, that of June 1741 to June 1747 and that of November 1774 to September 1780, were censured as having been prematurely dissolved and so was even the parliament of May 1768 to September 1774.   For example, among critics of the dissolution of June 1747 Thomas Potter, member for St. Germans and son of the Archbishop of Canterbury, declared in the Commons that parliament was being dissolved 'in a new and unprecedented, I had almost said unconstitutional, manner'.   The King, for his part, thought it necessary to justify the dissolution, and did so by stating that as parliament 'would necessarily determine, in a short time, and as nothing will give so much weight and credit to our affairs abroad in the present conjuncture, as to show the dependence I have upon the affections of my people ; I have judged it expedient speedily to call a new parliament'.   Criticism of the 1774 dissolution was more widespread, though the dissolved parliament was nearer the end of its permitted life.   The chief fear of the critics was that expressed by the author of *The History of Lord North's administration*, published in 1781.   'As this was a very unexpected measure', he wrote, 'because an unusual exertion of the regal prerogative, no similar instance having happened for almost one thirty years, it gave the ministry great advantages in the election of members.'[1]   In April 1780 Dunning tried to forestall a premature dissolution by moving for an address to the King, asking him 'not to dissolve the parliament, or prorogue the present session' until satisfactory measures of economical reform had been passed.   Although it was pointed out that an attempt to restrain the King from dissolving parliament was unprecedented and unconstitutional, Dunning's motion was only lost by 203 votes to 254.   The closeness of the vote made a dissolution, from the government's point of view, more desirable.   Parliament was prorogued in August, and its dissolution in September by proclamation, while it was still prorogued, 'acted', in the words of the *Annual Register*, 'like a thunderclap'.   The criticism of the dissolutions of 1747, 1774, and 1780 is a measure of the strength of the convention which grew upon the Septennial Act.   The fact that this criticism was directed against the dissolution of parliaments which had, at most, only about a year of their permitted life left to them, explains the violence of the attacks on the more seriously premature dissolutions of the period between 1784 and 1832.

The Septennial Bill was introduced on 10 April 1716, and, like so many previous Bills dealing with the duration of parliament, it originated in the House of Lords.   On this occasion, the Bill's place of origin was a sign that it was a measure approved by the government.   It dealt with a single problem, that of the maximum life of parliament.   It therefore repealed only the clause of the Triennial Act of 1694 which provided that parliaments should

[1] Bodleian Library, *Godwyn Pamphlets*, vol. 1938, p. 165.   This was not North's opinion : indeed, he feared that the government might find itself less strong in the new House than 'if we were at the natural end of the Parliament. . . . Many good consequences will result from a sudden dissolution, but some seats in the House of Commons will probably be lost by it' (North to George III, 27 September 1774. *Correspondence of George III*, ed. Fortescue, iii. 134).   The 'good consequences' are accurately described in *The History* as the avoidance of 'the framing of such popular acts, as constantly take place in the last session of a parliament' (*op. cit.* p. 166).

not last for more than three years, and provided instead that 'this present Parliament, and all Parliaments that shall at any future Time hereafter be called, assembled or held, shall and may respectively have continuance for seven years, and no longer . . . unless this present, or any such Parliament hereafter to be summoned, shall be sooner dissolved by His Majesty, his Heirs or Successors'. No reference was made either to the problem of the intervals between parliaments or to the problem of frequent parliaments, and the provision in the Triennial Act of 1694 that parliaments should be 'holden' at least once in every three years therefore remained. There was some opposition to the Bill in both Houses, but it passed both Houses fairly easily : the voting on the third reading was 69 to 36 in the Lords, and 264 to 121 in the Commons.

The government's wish to extend the life of the existing parliament, which met in March 1715, and to avoid an impending general election in unquiet times, 'when a restless and Popish Faction are designing and endeavouring to renew the Rebellion within this Kingdom, and an Invasion from abroad', was of course political. It was argued at the time, and it has often been argued since, that no parliament can constitutionally 'prolong its own life' without reference to the electorate. This argument has always been a natural one for opponents of the Bill to use, but it is not a good one. By the Triennial Act of 1694 a parliament had, without reference to the electorate, restricted its own life, by providing a date by which it must be dissolved, as well as restricting the life of future parliaments. Equally, a parliament could unquestionably, without reference to the electorate, have repealed the Triennial Act and so regained an indefinite maximum life both for itself and for all future parliaments. Moreover, parliament did not in fact prolong its own life in 1716 but merely restricted its life rather less severely by extending the period within which the King must dissolve it and future parliaments. This extension was certainly legal. It is not easy to claim that it was not also constitutional for parliament to modify a restriction imposed by a previous parliament on the King's prerogative, and to do so immediately, since the electorate had not previously been considered to be in any way concerned with the duration of the parliament they elected at the King's command. It is true that opponents of the Bill claimed that 'the people chose their present representatives only for three years and they would be no longer the Parliament chosen by the people if they are continued without their consent'. This argument, however, was based on the validity of the Triennial Act, and so did not accord well with their other argument, that 'the Triennial Act gave the crown a greater prerogative in this matter than it had before by the custom of Parliaments', and that 'we ought not for a little necessity or conveniency alter the fundamental laws of the nation and give up the liberty of the subject'. For it seems that by 'the fundamental laws of the nation' the opponents of the Bill after all meant, as did the twenty-four dissentient peers, not the Triennial Act but the statutes of Edward III and the 'ancient and primitive practice of frequent and new parliaments'. This spoilt their argument about the Triennial Act. In any case, the supporters of the Bill had a good answer to both arguments: 'the Triennial Act is but of twenty years standing and therefore to take it away can be no breach of our constitution unless the making it had been one. . . . And as to the ancient custom of calling Parliaments every year that was for the convenience of subjects themselves who wanted to be at their own houses in the country.' The first contention is valid; the second at least shows how unreal it was to appeal for justification to the statutes of Edward III.

Quite apart from the question of the life of the existing parliament, there were good reasons for an extension of the maximum life of future parliaments, and, from the constitutional point of view, this was the real importance of the Septennial Act. Even more important, but not inevitable, was the Septennial convention. For it was this convention which endeared to upholders of the Commons' independence an Act which, when it was passed, seemed to some of them more like a strengthening of the King's prerogative. To a few members of the Commons in 1716 the Septennial Bill was obnoxious, quite apart from its content, because it originated in the House of Lords. 'It is sent from the Lords', said Shippen, 'and as it clearly relates to ourselves I shall apprehend it inconsistent with our honour to receive it.' The main opposition in the Commons, however, came from those who feared that the Bill would tighten the King's hold upon the Commons, and strengthen him by adding a 'standing parliament' to a standing army. It was urged too that the Bill would free members from the frequent and salutary criticism of their constituents, increase the value of seats, and so increase the size of the bribes offered for votes. For the most part, supporters of the Bill agreed with its opponents that there had been electoral corruption in the period between 1694 and 1716, but, while supporters of the Bill attributed this corruption to the Triennial Act, their opponents maintained that the way to diminish corruption was not to reduce but to increase the number of general elections. That, in spite of these forebodings, the Septennial Act so soon came to be extolled as the chief guarantee of the Commons' independence, and the foundation of the constitution, was due to the rapid growth of the Septennial convention, by which the Commons seemed, at last, to have achieved a normal, regular and long life of their own, and the King's power of making and unmaking parliaments at his will seemed to have been checked without having been abolished. Speaker Onslow's opinion, 'That the passing of the septennial bill formed the era of the emancipation of the British house of commons from its former dependence on the crown and the house of lords', was echoed by many champions of the Commons' independence.

The belief that the independence of the Commons was bound up with the Septennial Act was the chief reason for the failure of attempts to repeal it, and to substitute a system of annual or triennial parliaments. These attempts sought to decrease the Commons' independence not in the interests of the King but in the interests of the electorate, who ought, it was said, to be able to change their representatives more frequently than once in every seven years. There were two recurrent demands : that members of parliament should be tied more tightly to their constituents, and that the statutes of Edward III should be regarded as applicable to eighteenth-century parliaments. The first demand was connected with the larger question of the relation between members and their constituents, and, in particular, whether members were bound either to consult their constituents about their conduct in parliament or to follow instructions issued to them by their constituents. The idea that members were bound in this way was generally regarded as an infringement of the Commons' independence no less dangerous than its infringement by the King. For example, every edition of Chamberlayne's *Present State of England* and *Present State of Great Britain*, from 1669 to 1755, included a 'Note, that although every Member of the Commons' House be chosen to serve for one particular County, City, or Borough, yet he serves for the whole Kingdom, and his Voice is equal to any other, his Power absolute to consent or dissent without ever acquainting those that sent him, or demanding their Assent, as the States-General of the United Netherlands are obliged to do in many cases.' The issue of instructions by the electors of Buckinghamshire and London at the general election of 1715, immediately before the passing of the Septennial Act, provoked much indignation.[1]   Before this, Chamberlayne's 'note' was followed by a sentence which might have seemed to qualify it : 'Yet are they to make it their special Care to promote the good of that County, City, or Burrough, for which they serve, and from which heretofore they usually did receive Instructions and Directions concerning their Grievances, Wants, etc.'   After 1716 this specific reference to members' care for their constituencies, and instructions formerly issued by them, was omitted.[2]   In this form, shorn of the qualifying sentence which followed it, Chamberlayne's 'note' expressed the orthodox eighteenth-century view of the relation between members and their constituents.   This view had been put forward in the 1680s by Algernon Sydney, whose *Discourses on Government* was first published in 1698 and was reprinted in 1763.   It was echoed in 1743 by John Perceval, second Earl of Egmont, who complained in *Faction detected by the Evidence of Facts* of the issue of instructions by the electors of London, Westminster, and other cities.[3]   Their

[1] The election addresses of February and March 1681, which purported to be instructions from constituents to candidates, provide an earlier example of an attempt by electors to bind their members to a particular policy.   But in this case the policy advocated — the exclusion of the Duke of York from the throne — did not originate with the constituents who put it forward.   This is probably true also of the Kentish Petition and Legion Letter of 1701, which were based on a similar idea : members of parliament were required to support a particular policy on the grounds that it was the policy of their 'Masters (for such are the People who chose you) . . . (as the person sent is less than the sender)' (*Parliamentary History*, v. 1253, 1256).

[2] It is significant that the second part of the sentence ('and from which heretofore they usually did receive Instructions and Directions concerning their Grievances, Wants, etc') was only added in 1679.

[3] These were the instructions issued after the fall of Walpole.   A selection (eighteen counties, twelve cities, fifteen boroughs) of the constituencies which issued them is given in *Parliamentary History*, xii. 416-17. All the instructing constituencies are said to have demanded 'the restoring of Triennial Parliaments'.   On the other hand, Sir John St. Aubyn, when seconding the motion for repealing the Septennial Act in 1734, had argued that 'remonstrances' from the electorate to parliament would be fewer if the electorate had 'more frequent opportunities of varying the choice of their representatives, that they may dismiss those who have unfaithfully withdrawn their attention from them' (*Parliamentary History*, ix. 402-3).

issue was due, he said, to 'a party of Malcontents, (who), assuming to themselves, though very falsely, the title of the People, claim with it a pretension which no people could have a right to claim, affecting a superiority to the whole Legislature, insolently taking upon themselves to dictate to all the three estates, in which the absolute power of the Government, by all the laws of this country, has indisputably resided ever since it was a Government'. Blackstone insisted that the purpose for which a member of parliament was elected, 'not barely to advantage his constituents, but the *common* wealth', made it essential that, once elected, he should be free of his constituents, and de Lolme almost repeats Chamberlayne's words : 'Those Deputies, though separately elected, do not solely represent the Town or County that sends them, as is the case with the Deputies of the United Provinces, or of the Swiss Cantons ; but, when once they are admitted, they represent the whole body of the Nation'. David Hume, who also looked at Holland as a warning, saw that a House of Commons bound by instructions would be a House transformed into a body of delegates backed by 'the immense power and riches . . . of all the Commons of Great Britain' ; if these 'were brought into the scale' the parliamentary balance could not subsist, for the King's influence over the Commons would be of no account in the face of the Commons' enormous power. Freedom from instructions was therefore a vital guarantee of the parliamentary balance, and 'an alteration in this particular would introduce a total alteration in our government'. The connection between the idea of instructions and the repeal of the Septennial Act is very evident both in the conduct and pretensions of the supporters of Wilkes [1] and

[1] For example, before the 1774 general election Lord Mahon, who stood for Westminster, promised the electors to work for the repeal of the Septennial Act in order 'to strengthen and encrease the due and necessary relation between the representative and constituent bodies', and Wilkes and Glyn, at their nomination as candidates for Middlesex, signed a

in the extra-parliamentary agitation for reform in 1780, and some of the 1780 reformers, citing Coke as authority, claimed that there was medieval precedent for the contention that members should not assent to proposals put to them in parliament until they had consulted their constituents.

In the same way the 1780 reformers invoked medieval precedent, and in particular the statutes of Edward III, to support their claim that, in the words of the Westminster sub-Committee, 'new parliaments to be holden once in every year were the antient usage'. This was indeed the contention of all would-be repealers of the Septennial Act, who praised the statutes of Edward III with something of the reverence accorded in the seventeenth century to Magna Carta as the corner-stone of English liberties. Two answers were made to the contention; the first denied that the reformers were correctly interpreting the statutes of Edward III, the second denied that the statutes were relevant to eighteenth-century political conditions. The first answer was made by Blackstone, who gave his opinion that the statutes of 4 Edward III and 36 Edward III placed upon the King, not the obligation to summon a new parliament every year, but the obligation to allow a parliament to sit at least once every year. The second answer was made by Earl Nugent, in 1780, in reply to a motion for frequent parliaments. The circumstances which the reformers wished to revive were, he pointed out, 'ages when the House of Commons was an insignificant part of the Constitution'. 'What', he asked, 'was it meant that parliament should be degraded to that state in

'solemn engagement' which included a promise 'to promote acts of the legislature for shortening the duration of parliaments'. Before the 1784 election Wilkes again pledged himself to raise the question of 'the shortening the duration of parliaments' very early in the new parliament, and asked the electors 'to believe that I shall be extremely desirous of receiving your instructions on every event of importance respecting my parliamentary conduct, if I am so happy as to have the late honourable relation to you renewed'.

which it was, when the service was so disagreeable that men were obliged to be paid for sitting and doing the public business ? When that business was so unwelcome, that there were frequent instances of persons begging to be disfranchised, in order to prevent their being sent up to parliament ?' It cannot be said that Blackstone was certainly either right or wrong, since in the fourteenth century, when single sessions were the rule, 'holding parliaments' meant, in practice, the same as 'summoning parliaments', but it is difficult not to sympathize with Nugent's mocking at the antiquarian attack on the Septennial Act.

A few reformers attacked the Act on other grounds, as an infringement of the Revolution Settlement. One of these was T. H B. Oldfield. In the *History of the Boroughs*, published in 1792, Oldfield maintained that 'extending parliaments . . . to a term of seven years is contrary to a positive declaration in this act (the Declaration of Rights) which says that parliaments ought to be held frequently', and that the Declaration of Rights was 'a compact the people made with the Prince of Orange, for admitting him, and the heirs of his body, to the possession of their throne'. The Septennial Act, therefore, 'was a forfeiture of one of the conditions by which the said King and his successors held their crown. For however sophists may pretend to explain, that the words *"hold frequently"* mean not any other than frequent sessions, yet it is evident that the expression of parliaments ought to be held frequently, implies the necessity of assembling new parliaments often. As there may be many sessions, and but one parliament in seven years, *holding parliaments frequently* cannot be applied to the frequent assembling of one, but the frequent choice of new parliaments. And this is still more positively expressed by the word *parliaments* being in the plural instead of singular. There is, therefore, not only a constitutional

right, but an express condition of compact, by which the
present crown is held for lessening the duration of parliaments to what they were originally.' These are stronger
arguments, though they do not entirely escape the pitfall
of the past, but they are not unanswerable. It is true that
for many people the Declaration of Rights was more than
a statute : it was a treaty between King and people. But
in de Lolme's opinion all statutes affecting the King's
prerogative of summoning and dissolving parliament were
treaties between King and people. The Septennial Act,
on this view, was in the nature of a revised treaty. Again,
for many people the demand for 'frequent parliaments'
had always meant, first and foremost, regularity of parliaments and security against the long absence of a parliament by dissolution or prorogation, and for them the
Septennial Act did not infringe the Revolution Settlement.
The practice of 'frequent and new parliaments', a phrase
first used not in the Declaration of Rights but in the
Triennial Act of 1694, had been found wanting, and the
Triennial Act, and indeed the Bill of Rights itself, since
the Declaration had been enacted in the form of a statute,
could be modified like any other statute. Finally, even
if it were admitted that the Septennial Act might, in 1716,
have infringed the Declaration of Rights, it could not be
repealed in 1792 merely on those grounds. For it had
abundantly proved its worth, as no other attempt to restrain
the King's prerogative in regard to the summoning and
dissolving of parliament had done.

The defenders of the Septennial Act had the best of
the argument, for they were realists, and based their
defence not on the past but on the present. They did
not argue about the interpretation of the statutes of
Edward III, and they did not, for the most part, answer
the charge that the Septennial Act was an infringement,
not of ancient statutes, but of a basic treaty between King
and people. Instead, they dipped into the past only to

point the contrast between the stability under the Septennial Act and the chaos and corruption under the Triennial Act, and they pointed further to the benefits which the Septennial Act had conferred, and especially to its part in making the Commons a regular part of the constitution and a strong counterweight to King and Lords. It is not surprising that their arguments prevailed. Although the Septennial Act was an obvious target for the opposition to Walpole, it proved difficult to enlist support for attacks on it. Many of the disaffected Whigs, for example, could not be persuaded to support the first motion for repeal, which was made by William Bromley, member for Warwick, in March 1734, even though it followed the failure of the attempt to dislodge Walpole on the question of the Excise Bill in 1733 and the failure of a Place Bill in February 1734. Moreover, Pulteney, who did support the motion, complained afterwards that the 'dictates of Bolingbroke' had been too evident in the debate. Walpole's defence of the Act was strong and effective. He denied that the Jacobite danger had been the 'chief motive for enacting that law', and he praised it as the great safeguard of mixed government, in which 'the monarchical, aristocratical and democratical forms of government are mixed and interwoven . . . so as to give us all the advantages of each, without subjecting us to the dangers and inconveniences of either'. The particular danger to which the constitution had been exposed by the Triennial Act, and rescued by the Septennial Act, was, he asserted, that of 'running too much into that form of government which is properly called democratical'. Triennial or annual parliaments were bound to be 'as wavering and unsteady as the people usually are', and 'by such frequent elections there would be so much power thrown into the hands of the people, as would destroy that equal mixture, which is the beauty of our constitution. . . . Therefore, in order to preserve our constitution, in order to preserve our falling

under tyranny and arbitrary power, we ought to preserve
that law, which I really think has brought our constitution
to a more equal mixture, and consequently to a greater
perfection than it was ever in before that law took place.'
The motion for repeal was defeated by 247 votes to 184.
Later attempts to repeal the Septennial Act and shorten
the duration of parliament called forth similar praises, and
motions for repeal were defeated in March 1742, in January 1745, and in 1758. In opposing the 1745 motion Sir
William Yonge praised the Septennial Act for having put
an end to the 'continual disturbances that would be
occasioned by frequent elections and the fluctuations in
all public measures that must necessarily ensue from a
frequent change of public magistrates or representatives',
and maintained that members of parliament could perform
their duty 'as inquisitors . . . as well in a septennial as
in an annual parliament, if the former meets regularly
once a year, and continue sitting until they have finished
all the material business before them'. The demand for
frequent elections, Yonge argued, suggested that members
of parliament were 'nothing more than the attornies of
the particular county, city, or borough, they respectively
represent' ; in reality each member was 'the servant, or,
if you like, the attorney of the people of England in general
. . . and there is therefore no greater absurdity in choosing
a representative for a long term of years than in choosing
a King or chief magistrate for a long term of years'. Again,
in 1780, in opposing one of the thirteen motions for annual
parliaments made by Alderman Sawbridge between 1771
and 1786, Burke, who had made his famous attack on the
principle of delegation at Bristol in 1774, asserted that
shorter parliaments would reduce members of parliament
to the status of 'canvassers at a perpetual election', destroy
the 'independency' secured to them by the Septennial
Act, and increase 'corruptibility' by 'removing the influence (of the Court) from the elected to the electors',

so strengthening 'a court influence already great and powerful in boroughs'.

(ii) THE COMPOSITION OF THE COMMONS

The second element in the framework of eighteenth-century government was the composition of the House of Commons. It gave rise to a second problem connected with the theme of the Commons' independence. The problem associated with the first element concerned the Commons as a body : how far could it have an independent, certain, and regular existence ? The problem associated with the second element concerned the House of Commons as a collection of individuals : how far could they be kept independent of the King and his ministers ? It seemed that they could not be so kept unless they were forbidden to hold crown offices or pensions or any other form of favour from the crown. The two problems, of the body and its members, were found together in Charles II's long parliament, which was thought to be servile partly because it was long and partly because many of its members held places and pensions from the crown. Both in this parliament and after it, therefore, proposals for shortening the life of parliament were often made at the same time as proposals for forbidding members of parliament to hold crown offices. The avowed object of both proposals was to secure and preserve the independence of parliament. The first problem was regarded by the Commons as peculiarly their concern, since dissolution destroyed the House of Commons while it merely adjourned the House of Lords : indeed, on these grounds, the Commons often showed resentment at attempts by the Lords to take the initiation in legislation affecting the life and dissolution of parliaments. The second problem obviously concerned the Commons alone : here the Lords seldom attempted to take the initiative, though they often tried to moderate the Commons' proposals. Thus the phrase 'independence of parliament' came to be generally used as the equivalent of 'independence of the House of Commons', just as the phrase 'member of parliament', first used to denote a member of the House of Commons in 1650, after Charles I's execution, retained this meaning after 1660 and was not again used in its original sense as a member of either House.

The idea that membership of parliament was not only an end in itself but also a stepping-stone to employment under the crown was, of course, not new. But its application in practice increased rapidly after 1660. The idea appealed to the King and his ministers because the distribution of crown patronage among members of parliament seemed to offer a means of organizing the unwieldy mass of government supporters in the House of Commons; it appealed to ambitious members of the House in search of a career; it appealed to less ambitious members because they were no longer paid for their services. At the same time, the House of Commons as a body became increasingly opposed to the idea that any of its members should be employed by or paid by the crown. There was thus created an irreconcilable conflict of interest between the House of Commons as a body and the House of Commons as a collection of individuals, and this conflict weakened the Commons and benefited the King by providing him with a much-needed bridge to the Commons.

To forbid members of parliament to hold office from the crown was, therefore, a policy inspired not by the theory of separation of powers but by the much older fear of the King's undermining of the Commons' independence. Advocates of the policy were agreed that members of parliament should forfeit their seats in the House if they accepted any office or pension from the Crown. Halifax, for example, wrote in the 1690s that 'a member of parliament, of all others, ought least to be exempted from the rule that no man should serve two masters. . . . It either giveth a real dependence upon the Government, which is inconsistent with the necessity there is that a Member of Parliament should be disengaged, or at least it hath the appearance of it, which maketh them not look like freemen, though they should have virtue enough to be so.' [1] On the other hand, there was disagreement on the question of whether members who accepted offices should be allowed to stand again for election to parliament. Some thought that it should lie with the constituencies to decide whether they were content to be represented by members who were also servants of the crown ; others thought the problem was not one for the constituencies but for the Commons, who might, if they wished, give particular members permission to accept office ; others thought that a crown servant was not in any circumstances a suitable member of the Commons, for, by accepting office, he had betrayed not only his trust from his constituents but also the idea of an independent House of Commons. Perhaps surprisingly, the first view, that the decision in each individual case should be left to the constituency, in the end prevailed.

Before 1689 the House of Commons attempted not to keep its members entirely away from the King's service but to impose conditions on their acceptance of office. In this the House did not succeed. The Bill introduced into the Commons in April 1675, and defeated on the motion to send it to committee, made acceptance of office conditional on the approval of the constituencies : members who accepted an office from the crown were to be required to vacate their seats but allowed to stand for re-election. 'Where an office is inconsistent with the service of

[1] 'Some Cautions offered to the Consideration of those who are to choose Members to serve in the ensuing Parliament', printed in Foxcroft, *Life and Letters of Halifax*, ii. 487.

the country in the person that has it', said Sir John Vaughan, member for Carmarthen, 'it is reasonable that place should choose another person, and where that place has no jealousy to think they shall not be well served, it is for the honour of the person to be chosen again.' On the other hand, the Resolution passed by the Commons on 30 December 1680 made acceptance of office conditional on the approval of the House. But parliament was dissolved within three weeks, and its two successors before 1689 had little chance to insist that the Resolution be observed. The more radical attempts in the 1690s to exclude placemen unconditionally from the House of Commons were also unsuccessful. They were closely associated with other proposals made in the 1690s with the object of safeguarding the independence of parliament: the Triennial Bills; proposals that members of parliament should be paid; attempts to regulate the conduct of elections; resolutions denying the right of peers either to vote or to interfere in parliamentary elections; attempts to prevent certain groups of crown officials from interfering in elections. The first of the Place Bills of the 1690s, the 'Self-denying bill' introduced in December 1692 by Sir Edward Hussey, provided for complete exclusion of placemen from the House of Commons: after January 1693 no office-holder should be capable of being elected and members who accepted offices were to lose their seats without possibility of being elected again. The Bill passed the House of Commons, but in the House of Lords, after the failure of an amendment permitting re-election, it was defeated by 47 votes to 45. The Protest entered by the defeated peers accepted the Commons' contention that the problem of placemen was peculiarly their concern: the fact that the King would 'never be capable' of 'too long continuing the parliament' was not considered to be sufficient ground for rejecting the Bill, for 'we have good reason to believe that the House of Commons would not have begun and passed a Bill of this nature, wherein the Members of their House are so particularly concerned, without having been fully satisfied in the reasons of it, and plainly convinced of the great need the people of *England* are in, at this time, of so just and wise a provision'. One of the arguments used by the opponents of the Bill in the Lords was that, if it passed, the King would be forced to prolong the existing parliament indefinitely, since any new one would be completely unmanageable. This argument led Shrewsbury, in January 1693, to introduce into the Lords a Bill 'for the frequent Meeting of Parliaments' — the Triennial Bill to which William refused his assent in February. The second Place Bill was introduced in December 1693. Its provisions were similar to those of the earlier Bill and again it passed the Commons. The Lords inserted an amendment, on the lines of the 1675 Bill, allowing members who vacated their seats as a result of acceptance of office to stand for re-election, and passed the Bill in this form. The Commons accepted the amendment, but William III refused his assent to the Bill. The Commons' representation to William, in January 1694, showed that they resented his refusal more than they had resented his rejection of other Bills : they decided, for example, against including in their representation an explicit reference to his rejection of the Triennial Bill, and contented themselves with an expression of regret that William had refused the royal assent to several public Bills, 'and, in particular, a Bill entitled "An Act touching free and impartial Proceedings in Parliament", which was made to redress a Grievance, and take off a Scandal relating to the Proceedings of your Commons in Parliament'. For the Place Bill, 'which tended so much to the clearing the Reputation of this House', was, above all else, the Commons' vindication of their expressed wish for independence, and its passing was a victory for the common interests of the House over the particular interests of its members.

The third Place Bill, introduced in 1695, came at a time when William was more popular, and, partly for this reason, it was rejected, by 142 votes to 95, in the Commons.

These early attempts by the House of Commons to prevent, or at least control, the 'winning over' of its members by the King coincided with a great increase in the number of government employees, as a result of the abandonment of farming as a method of collecting the Customs duties in 1671, the Excise duties in 1683, the Hearth duties in 1684, and other duties rather later. The reform in the method of collection, and the consequent employment of something like 8000 revenue officers, was criticized, throughout the eighteenth century, less on its merits than on the ground that it represented a great increase in the volume of government patronage. For an increase in government patronage was a threat to the independence of parliament because it provided more loaves and fishes with which individual members of parliament could be won over to support the crown. In this way, Hatsell observed, 'a new system of power and influence arose, not known, or in very small degree, before the Revolution'.

Although the general Place Bills of the 1690s failed, and none was introduced after 1705, simultaneous attempts to exclude revenue officers from the House of Commons succeeded. An Act of 1693 forbade members of the House of Commons, other than Commissioners of the Treasury and of Customs and Excise, to be concerned directly or indirectly in the management or collection of taxes granted by the Act itself or by future Acts. This equating of the Commissioners of Customs and Excise — the most lucrative duties — with the Commissioners of the Treasury only lasted until 1699: Commissioners and officers of the Board of Excise were excluded by an Act of 1699 and Commissioners and officers of the Board of Customs by an Act of 1701. Officers engaged in the management of smaller revenue duties were excluded later in the eighteenth century — mainly by the Succession to the Crown Act of 1707 and the Place Act of 1742. In its effect on the composition of the House of Commons the importance of the exclusion of revenue officers, high and low, was that they were the largest group of eighteenth-century government employees. Their exclusion can therefore be hailed as the first step towards the exclusion of civil servants from parliament, though in practice the step did not touch the greater problem of freeing them from politics. The second step was a Place Act of 1742 which debarred clerks and deputies of all the main government departments from sitting in the House of Commons. This second step was more important, since it applied exclusion not only to revenue officers but to ordinary civil servants. At the same time, it was more limited, for it applied only to lesser civil servants : the secretaries and under-secretaries of the same departments continued to sit in the Commons, and the greatest of them, the Secretary to the Treasury, was not excluded until 1867.

The necessity of defining the royal prerogative more exactly, against the Hanoverian succession, again made it possible to try to safeguard the Commons' independence by excluding all office-holders from the House. General Place Bills of 1700, 1702, and 1704 failed, as did two more moderate ones of 1705, and the Commons' Resolution of December 1702 excluding placemen from the House was entirely ineffective. But a clause in the Act of Settlement provided that, if and when Anne died without issue, 'no person who has an Office or Place of Profit under the King or receives a pension from the Crown shall be capable of serving as a member of the House of Commons'. This clause was a statutory embodiment of the idea that no member of parliament should serve two masters; if the clause had come into effect it would have prevented the development of the most important connection between

King and Commons in the eighteenth century and made renewed conflict between them inevitable. It is true that, if the clause had been long in force, it would have prevented members of the government from sitting in the House of Commons. But this is less relevant, partly because it was not the purpose of the clause, and partly because, since the clause was never tested in practice, it must be judged by its intention. The Privy Council clause in the Act of Settlement, not the Place clause, was directed towards the problem of the executive at ministerial level. The Place clause was not intended as a step towards a separation of powers, to be achieved by excluding the King's ministers from the Commons; it was intended as a step towards the independence of the House of Commons, to be achieved by excluding the King's influence from all its members. The clause would, in practice, have affected very few ministers, for very few sat in the Commons; the fact that exclusion of ministers would have removed a potential method of controlling them was not apparent in 1701. This fact might well have affected the Commons' later policy, but it could hardly have affected their then policy of excluding placemen.

The Place clause in the Act of Settlement, like the Bill rejected by William III in 1693, was a victory for the advocates of the independence of the Commons, one of 'those victories which', in de Lolme's words, 'the Parliament from time to time gains over itself'. The particular expression of the victory was, however, the outcome, not of a reasoned consideration of the constitutional problem of whether parliamentary monarchy required a link or overlap in personnel between King and Commons, but, rather, of party conflicts. In the past the Whigs had demanded Place Bills; it was the Tories who pressed for the Place clause in the Act of Settlement, and they did so not because they had changed their views about the relation between King and Commons but because they wanted the Hanoverians to be weak kings. Indeed, the limitations imposed by the clause seemed, Burnet thought, 'so extravagant, as should quite change the form of our government, and render the Crown titular and precarious'. Many Whigs disliked the clause, believing that if the prerogative were clipped to this extent the Hanoverians might refuse the throne, and for this reason the next parliament, which met in June 1705 and contained a large Whig majority, repealed the clause and substituted for it a more moderate provision.

The modification of the Place clause in the Act of Settlement was incorporated first in the Succession to the Crown Act, 1705, and, after the Union with Scotland, in the Succession to the Crown Act, 1707. The modification, like the original clause, was largely the product of party fortunes : it reflected the fact that the Whigs were strong enough to insist not only that the Hanoverians should be less limited than the Tories wished, but also that the limitations should come into effect during Anne's reign and not apply only to the Hanoverians.

The idea of complete exclusion of all office-holders was abandoned : instead offices were divided into two categories, and the idea of conditional acceptance of office was revived. Clause 24 of the 1707 Act provides that no one holding a 'new' office (one created after the passing of the 1705 Act) or any one of a list of specified offices [1] shall be capable 'of being elected or of sitting or voting' [2] in the House of Commons. Clause 25 provides that if a member of parliament accepts 'any Office of Profit from

[1] Commissioner, Sub-Commissioner, Secretary, and Receiver of Prizes ; Comptroller of Army Accounts ; Commissioner of Transports, of Sick and Wounded, for Wine Licenses, of the Navy in the Out Ports ; Agent of a Regiment ; Governor and Deputy Governor of any of the Plantations ; Pensioner during Pleasure.

[2] This is a new phrase. Previous disqualifications applied only to 'service' in the House of Commons — that is, office-holders were not debarred from election, but they could not sit and vote unless they resigned their office (cf. the Acts excluding revenue officers, the Act of Settlement).

the Crown' he shall automatically forfeit his seat but shall be allowed to stand for re-election. The intention of the Act is perhaps not made clear in the wording of these clauses : there can be no doubt that the Act intends to draw a distinction between 'old' offices on the one hand and 'new' and specified offices on the other, but the nature of the intended distinction is obscure. Clause 25 implies that members of parliament who accept 'new' and specified offices, and not only those who accept 'old' offices, may stand for re-election ; modern commentators on the clause point out that this would cut across the division of offices into two categories, and maintain that, for this reason, clause 25 must be interpreted as if 'any office' meant 'any old office'.[1]

This interpretation of the Act was not, however, consistently applied in practice. Members who held specified offices were re-elected and allowed to sit, apparently without question, in the parliament which passed the Act. Later in the century men who held 'new' offices were allowed to sit, and although some at least of these 'new' office-holders were challenged, the Commons, instead of automatically expelling them, debated the question of their capacity to sit. In this way, by asserting their right to decide that a particular 'new' office should be treated as if it were an 'old' office,[2] the Commons admitted, by

[1] For example, Erskine May states that section 25 'clearly must be so limited (*i.e.* to "old" offices) as it would otherwise be in direct conflict with the preceding section' (*Parliamentary Practice*, 1947 edition, ed. Campion, p. 201) and Anson considers that section 25 'must be construed to refer to *old* offices, otherwise it would repeal a part of S. 24' (*Law and Custom of the Constitution*, vol. i, ed. Gwyer, p. 85). Earlier commentators do not make this gloss : Blackstone, for example, merely states that 'if any member accepts an office under the crown, except an office in the army or navy accepting a new commission, his seat is void ; but such member is capable of being re-elected' (*Commentaries on the Laws of England*, i. 176).

[2] An early example is the office of Commissioner for arranging trade with France. In March 1714 Joseph Martyn, member for Hastings, accepted this office and was re-elected by his constituents ; in April the House negatived a motion that it was a new office. Again, in 1775, the House resolved that John Maitland, member for North Berwick, was 'eligible to serve in Parliament, notwithstanding his being in possession of

implication, that the date of creation of offices was not a sufficient criterion for distinguishing between them. This *ad hoc* treatment of 'new' offices adds to the difficulty of giving a precise definition of the intention of the 1705 Act. The Act used three devices to modify the complete exclusion prescribed by the Act of Settlement : re-election ; specific exclusion of holders of certain existing offices ; exclusion of holders of 'new' offices as a protection against the possible creation of large numbers of them. The third of these devices, unlike the first and second, is not based on principle, and it is therefore hardly surprising that, in practice, it was not rigidly applied. Indeed, it may be that the apparently loose drafting of clause 25 was not entirely accidental.

Unlike the Place clause in the Act of Settlement, which was to apply only to the Hanoverians, the provisions of clauses 24 and 25 of the Succession to the Crown Act were to operate from the end of the parliament which was then sitting. On 29 April 1707 the members of this parliament were declared by royal proclamation to be members of the first parliament of Great Britain, and on 10 November a Resolution of the House of Commons applied clauses 24 and 25 to this parliament. Seven members forfeited their seats immediately as a result of the Resolution, and three more forfeited them before the dissolution in April 1708. Of these, six held specified offices under clause 24 — three Commissioners, one Sub-Commissioner and one Receiver of Prizes, one Commissioner of Sick and Wounded — and all of them except the last were re-elected.

Conditional acceptance of office, the requirement that members accepting office should seek re-election if they

the office of Clerk of the Pipe in the Exchequer in Scotland, at the time of his election'. Later, statutes creating new offices usually declared their holders eligible or ineligible — for example, in 1797 the Commissioners for the redemption or sale of the Land Tax were declared eligible, and in 1810 only one of the Commissioners of Woods and Forests was declared eligible — and this practice continued through the nineteenth century.

wished to remain in the House, was the cause of many by-elections and some defeats both in the eighteenth century and in the nineteenth century. It meant that members of parliament chosen as ministers and junior ministers, as well as members offered lesser offices or sinecures as a reward for their services to the King, might find themselves rejected by their constituents and, unless able to obtain election in another constituency, thrust out of the House of Commons. This was obviously inconvenient from the government's point of view, and it provided another reason why ministers were in the main chosen from or sent to the House of Lords, and one reason why junior ministers and rising politicians more often sat for close boroughs than for counties or for popular boroughs with a wide franchise. From the Commons' point of view, however, the requirement of re-election was a protection against the constantly encroaching influence of the crown, and a check on its enslavement of the whole body of the Commons. Attempts were made, immediately after the first Reform Bill,[1] in the 1850s during the agitation for further parliamentary reform, and at the time of the second Reform Bill, to abolish the requirement of re-election on appointment to ministerial office, on the grounds that, since time and reform had rendered the influence of the crown harmless, re-election had become an old-fashioned and unnecessary restriction on the crown's choice of servants. The attempts failed, and, except that the second Reform Act allowed members to transfer from one to another of certain specified ministerial offices without re-election, the requirement remained in force until 1926.

The irksomeness and tenacity of the requirement of

[1] Cf. Sir Robert Heron's motion of 1 May 1834 for a Bill to abolish the requirement of re-election on appointment to certain ministerial offices, and Edward Lytton Bulwer's amendment proposing that certain ministers and junior ministers should be *ex-officio* members of the House of Commons 'but without the privilege of voting, unless returned by the suffrages of a constituency'. Both motion and amendment were withdrawn (*Hansard*, 3rd series, xxiii. 382-97).

re-election enhanced the value to the King and his ministers of a small group of ten or twelve office-holders, secretaries and under-secretaries of the main government departments, who were not mentioned in the 1707 Act and who escaped its provisions because, being appointed by their ministers and not by the King, their places were regarded as not being 'offices under the crown'. These men were in their own right important administrative officers ; their importance was increased because, after the 1707 Act, they held the only offices which could be accepted unconditionally by members of parliament.

It cannot be pretended that, in practice, the 1707 Act had more than a limited effect on the composition of the Commons. There were not many specified offices, and the ineligibility of holders of 'new' offices was not of great importance because, even by the end of the century, there were not many of them and, in practice, they were not all excluded. The provision about re-election was more important, but although it influenced the distribution of offices it did not effect more than a small reduction in the number of office-holders who sat in the House. Some of the reasons why few members appointed to office failed to secure re-election to parliament were of course unconnected with the 1707 Act. In the parliament of 1715–22, the first septennial parliament, 107 members accepted offices which entailed vacation of seats, and 82 of these were re-elected. During this parliament, which saw five changes of administration, the number of appointments to office was large, but even so they concerned only two-fifths of the 271 places, including army and navy offices, held by members of the Commons in 1715. In the first and second parliaments of George II's reign, when the appointments to office concerned only about one-quarter of the total places held by members of the House, the proportion of re-elections to appointments was much the same : in the 1727–34 parliament there were 63 appointments and 50 re-elections, in the 1734–41 parliament 54 appointments and 39 re-elections. This remained true later in the century: the number of appointments varied from parliament to parliament, largely according to the number of changes of administration, but the proportion of re-elections was high and fairly constant.

Five Place Bills were introduced between 1707 and 1715. All were less moderate than the 1707 Act, and all were rejected in the House of Lords. The position in the early years of George I's reign was therefore defined, apart from the Acts excluding revenue officers, by the 1707 Act. In 1716, with the passing of an Act excluding from the House of Commons pensioners for a term of years, the period of almost annual Place Bills came to an end and the period of consolidation began. The influence of the King over the House of Commons had been checked but not removed; the independence of the House of Commons had been furthered, but not certainly secured, by the application of the requirement of re-election to members accepting all but a handful of offices. This requirement, by enabling a large number of members of the Commons to hold places of some kind, made it possible for the King's ministers to use the King's patronage as an aid to the management of the King's supporters in the House of Commons, and so provided the essential basis for co-operation between King and Commons. It is more than a convenience of dating that the 1716 Place Act should so nearly coincide with the Septennial Act. The one was almost the last definition by the Commons of the extent of the King's influence over the composition of the House; the other defined the extent of the King's power of keeping an influenced House in existence. Taken together, they provided, for the first time, a stable statutory basis for a working relationship between a limited King and a limited House of Commons.

The advocates of the independence of parliament from

crown influence were concerned only with the elected House of Commons; they were not interested in the independence of the hereditary House of Lords, which indeed they rather regarded as a threat to their own independence. Yet it was possible for the King to influence the composition of the House of Lords in ways in which, after 1689, he could not influence that of the Commons. He might try to influence the Commons by distributing places to its members, or by exerting pressure at elections, but his claim to add new members had been challenged in Charles II's reign and was not made afterwards. His right to alter the composition of the House of Lords directly could only be challenged by restricting his right to create peers. The number of lay peers in the House of Lords increased from 56 in 1601 to 142 in 1661 and 161 at the beginning of Anne's reign. Anne created sixteen peers, four in 1704 and twelve in 1712, in order to facilitate acceptance of the Peace of Utrecht, the Union with Scotland added sixteen elected Scottish peers and George I created about twenty peers in the first four years of his reign. These increases, partly offset by extinctions, brought the size of the House of Lords in 1719 to 218 : 176 lay peers, 16 Scottish peers, and 26 bishops.

At the beginning of March 1719 the House of Lords passed Resolutions approving the principle that the number of lay peers should be fixed by statute. The immediate motive behind the government's wish to restrict the King's prerogative of creating peers was, as with the Septennial Act, partly political, but many peers supported the attempt for reasons similar to those of the Commons when they protested against Charles II's grant of representation to Newark. These peers were not unsupported outside parliament. In January 1716 John Toland had maintained that 'the deadliest blow which was ever struck at the vitals of Parliament, has been the creating *a whole dozen of Peers* in one day, by the late Queen, while a most material Question was depending in the upper House', and hoped that 'the present Parliament will restore the Constitution, by doing something equally remarkable and effectual, both to put an eternal brand on that infamous action, and to secure Parliaments ever for the future from any such danger'. The King was persuaded to support the proposal, though his support seems to have surprised even its friends, and was explained away by its opponents as due to his lack of understanding of the constitution. Accordingly, he informed the House of Lords that 'he had so much at heart the settling the peerage of the whole kingdom, on such a foundation as might secure the freedom and constitution of parliament in all future ages, that he was willing his prerogative should stand not in the way of so great and necessary a work'. The Commons, however, so zealous in defence of their own independence, had little sympathy with the Lords' attempt to secure theirs. Indeed, the Commons were not even willing to regard the grant of a peerage to a commoner as part of the sinister use of crown influence, since such a grant removed the commoner from the House of Commons, while the grant of a place or pension left him there. On the contrary, the Commons opposed the proposal to fix the number of lay peers on the grounds that it would weaken the royal prerogative, increase the power and independence of the Lords, and so upset the balance of the constitution. The opposition of the Commons has been cited as an example of how the eighteenth-century constitution preserved itself by a system of checks and balances. This is only partly true : in face of an attempt by one of the balanced trio of King, Lords, and Commons to increase its power, the other two should have united against it. But although it was left to the Commons alone to defend what Oxford called 'the brightest gem of the crown', their defence was enough to save it.

A Bill was introduced into the House of Lords on

14 April 1719, by the Duke of Somerset, providing that the existing number of English peers should not be increased by more than six, and that the sixteen representative Scottish peers should be replaced by twenty-five hereditary ones. The object of the Bill was stated to be the preservation of the dignity of the peerage, and it was argued that since peerages became extinct so frequently the King's prerogative would not be seriously affected. The Bill did not meet with much opposition in the Lords, but it was postponed, before its third reading, in the face of severe attacks by pamphleteers, including Walpole and Steele, and in the press, opposition from Scotland, and expected hostility in the Commons. On 25 November, at the beginning of the next session, the Bill was introduced again. It passed the House of Lords easily, and it is clear that, in spite of opposition out of doors, Stanhope and Sunderland did not expect defeat in the Commons. It seems that, during the recess, Stanhope seriously considered the idea of repealing the Septennial Act, in the hope that the Commons might more easily accept the Peerage Bill if they were relieved of the limit on their existence. This offer was perhaps unlikely to win over the Commons. In any case, Newcastle insisted that an attempt to repeal the Septennial Act would increase rather than decrease opposition to the Peerage Bill in the Commons, and the offer was not made. In the event, the success of the opposition in the Commons was due primarily to Walpole. The Bills' easy passage in the House of Lords was sufficient in itself, Walpole thought, 'to inspire some jealousy in the Commons ; for it must be obvious, that whatever the Lords gain, must be acquired at the loss of the Commons, and the diminution of the regal prerogative'. This was, Walpole argued, a vital interest of the Commons and the strongest argument against the Bill, that it 'would endanger our excellent constitution ; for as there is a due balance between the

67

three branches of the legislature, it will destroy that balance, and consequently subvert the whole constitution, by causing one of the three powers, which are now dependent on each other, to preponderate in the scale'. Moreover, he insisted that the Commons had no need to fear the King's prerogative in so far as it related to the Lords : the King's unfettered right to create peers might weaken the House of Lords, but it could only tend to strengthen the Commons. After an eight-hour debate the motion to commit the Bill was defeated by 269 votes to 177.

So the size of the House of Lords, and the King's prerogative of adding to it, remained undefined by statute, and Walpole proved to be right in thinking that this would in the end strengthen the Commons. Nevertheless, the defeat of the Peerage Bill was far from reducing the House of Lords to a position of little account. In fact, the size of the House of Lords was little changed until the large peerage creations during the younger Pitt's administrations, and in 1783 the House was slightly smaller than it might have been if the Peerage Bill had become law. In theory, the Lords remained, like King and Commons, part of the parliamentary balance, and their power was a reflection and a guarantee of mixed government. Indeed, in one sense the Lords were the most vital part of the balance just because they were the least powerful, for they were, to quote Edward Wortley Montagu, 'placed in the middle of the balance, to prevent the Regal Scale from preponderating to Despotism or Tyranny ; or the Democratical to Anarchy and its consequences'. The position of the Lords in practice was not as widely removed from their position in theory as the encroachments of the Commons, particularly in the sphere of financial control, might suggest. For the power of the House of Lords, like that of the House of Commons, had two aspects : it consisted not only in its power as a body but in the position and influence of the peers as individuals. Although for the

House of Commons this division was a source of weakness, since it introduced a conflict of interest between the body and its members, with the House of Lords the division was a source of strength, for there was no conflict of interest between the House and the peers. As a body the House of Lords was certainly weakened as a result of the constitutional developments of the seventeenth and early eighteenth centuries, and the defeat of the Peerage Bill might well seem the defeat of its last attempt to encroach on the powers of either King or Commons. On the other hand, the powers of the House of Lords which derived from the territorial standing of its members, from the influence of individual peers over the electorate and over members of the House of Commons, and from the fact that most ministers were peers, were greater in the eighteenth than in the seventeenth century. Because of the extent of these indirect powers, the strength of the House of Lords in the eighteenth century in relation both to King and to Commons, was insignificant compared with the influence of its individual members over both.

(iii) THE KING'S REVENUE

The third element in the framework of eighteenth-century government, the King's revenue, is associated not with the degree of the Commons' independence of the King, as are the first and second elements, but with the degree of the King's independence of the Commons. In the period 1689–1716 steps were taken to relate the King's revenue more accurately to his commitments. This improvement in the King's financial position, however, made him more and not less dependent on parliament, for it was accompanied not only by the establishment of parliamentary control over the spending of the revenue granted to him by parliament, but also by an increase in the proportion of revenue which he obtained from parliament.

At the same time, parliamentary control was extended both over the raising of money by borrowing and over the spending of money so raised. The extended control over the raising of the King's revenue, and the new control over its expenditure, affected the King's prerogative of summoning and dissolving parliament, for it ensured that parliament should meet every year and it ended the possibility of long intervals between parliaments. So, in the sense that financial developments brought annual sessions and ensured that the summoning of a parliament should not be long delayed after the dissolution of its predecessor, this third element in the framework of eighteenth-century government is closely connected with the first, the life of the Commons. It is also connected with the second element, the composition of the Commons. For the tighter control was exercised not by parliament as a whole but primarily by the Commons, and this increased the strength and independence of the Commons both in relation to the King and in relation to the House of Lords. Again, the Commons' financial control is linked with the ascendancy of the First Lord of the Treasury, and with his management of the Commons by the distribution of the King's patronage to members of parliament.

The financial developments of the period 1689–1716 are not connected only indirectly with the achievement of a balance between King and Commons. They contributed directly to this balance by establishing a position of financial equilibrium, in which the King's income was not only fixed by parliament but guaranteed to him by parliament, and in which public expenditure was controlled partly by parliament and partly by the King, while the King's private expenditure remained wholly outside parliament's control. This financial balance between King and Commons was based, as was the constitutional balance between them, partly on statute and partly on convention, but it owed more to statute. The financial balance, shaken in 1782 and again in the early nineteenth century, was not finally destroyed until 1830. Its destruction, compared with the destruction of the constitutional balance, was simple : the Commons gained what the King lost.

The first step towards the achievement of the financial balance between King and Commons was based not on statute but on the vindication of claims made by the Commons. Since 1625 money Bills had been phrased in the form of a grant to the King, not from parliament, but from the Commons, with the advice and consent of the Lords. In the 1660s the Commons insisted that money Bills must always be introduced into the House of Commons, and in the 1670s the Commons further claimed that money Bills could not be amended in the House of Lords. The Lords' protests were unsuccessful, and in 1678 the Commons incorporated both claims in a Resolution. This claim that parliament's control of the King's revenue, like parliament's life and parliament's composition, was peculiarly the concern of the Commons, was never in the period 1660–1832 incorporated in statute ; but it was, in practice, conceded by the Lords before 1689, and they were not able seriously to challenge it again before 1832. Parliament's statutory gains in financial control between 1689 and 1832 were therefore in effect the Commons' gains.

In 1660 the public revenue was, as it always had been, entirely the same as the King's revenue, and this position was not changed before 1689. Between 1660 and 1689 the King was dependent on parliament for only a part of his revenue, and he was not accountable to parliament for the spending of any of it. In time of peace the King was expected to defray the expenses of government out of his ordinary revenue, and he was not expected to ask for extraordinary revenue except in time of war or preparations for war. Over borrowing, by means of which the King was free to supplement his ordinary and extraordinary revenue, parliament had no control. Indeed, parliament's

control over extraordinary revenue was limited to the author-
ization of its collection : the proceeds of taxes so authorized
were spent without any reference to parliament.

Before 1689 the Commons had made occasional attempts to ensure that money granted for extraordinary
purposes, and raised by taxes, was spent for the purpose
for which it had been asked. In William's reign, however, the Commons regularly began to state, either in the
Bill granting a tax or in a separate appropriation Bill, the
specific purpose for which the money collected was to be
used, and made some attempt to ensure that it was so
used. This was of fundamental constitutional importance,
for it was the first step towards parliamentary control of
public expenditure. The position then achieved lasted
until 1787, when, with the establishment of the Consolidated Fund, the system of appropriating each tax was
superseded by the simpler system of appropriating a
specific sum for each object of expenditure. Control was
made more effective by the system, which began in William's reign and became regular in the early eighteenth
century, of presenting to the House of Commons each
year estimates showing how it was proposed to spend the
money asked for the services which parliament supplied.
These estimates, prepared by the government department
concerned, were discussed, and often reduced, in Committee of Supply. On the other hand, attempts made in
William III's reign and in Anne's reign to superimpose
upon the Exchequer system of audit a parliamentary audit,
conducted by Commissions of Public Accounts composed
of members of parliament, were not effective and no
similar attempt was made in George I's reign.

Although the King's ordinary revenue continued after
1689 to be spent without reference to parliament, the
extent of parliamentary control over public expenditure
was further increased by the fact that the inadequacy of the
ordinary revenue led parliament not to add to it but to

reduce the King's commitments. After the Peace of Rys-
wick William III did not provide for military and naval
expenditure out of his ordinary revenue : this responsibility was assumed by parliament and provided for by
money voted each year by parliament, and the spending of
the money so voted was subject to parliamentary control.

This large increase in the field of expenditure controlled by parliament, which was also the first real step
towards the separation of the King's private expenditure
from public government expenditure, inaugurated a period
of balance between King and Commons, in which public
expenditure was controlled partly by the King and partly
by the Commons. The balance was shifted in the early
nineteenth century: in 1816 when deficiencies in certain
departmental fee funds began to be made good from money
specially granted by parliament instead of from the Civil
List, as had happened since 1810, and, less seriously, in 1802
and 1816 when various payments to members of the royal
family, some previously paid from the Civil List, became
charges on the Consolidated Fund. The final step was taken
in 1830. A Select Committee of the House of Commons
then appointed to examine the charges on the Civil List
Revenues laid down the principle that 'the Civil List should
be applied only to such expenses as affect the dignity and
state of the Crown and the personal comfort of Their
Majesties', and recommended that steps be taken to put
'expenses which are, in reality, the expenses of the Civil
Government of the State' under parliamentary control.
The recommendation was accepted, and the Civil List Act
of 1831 relieved the Civil List of its last great public
charges, the salaries of ministers and the expenses of civil
government departments.

The achievement, at the end of the seventeenth century,
of a balance between King and Commons in the control of
public expenditure was accompanied by the achievement
of a position in which parliament guaranteed to the King

F   73

a fixed annual income. The size of the income required by the King was estimated by parliament in 1660 and on several occasions during the succeeding reigns. Not until 1715, however, did parliament guarantee to the King the amount estimated, by undertaking to supplement, if necessary, the amount actually collected. The rule that if the amount collected exceeded the estimate the surplus should be surrendered was abandoned under George II, but the benefits of this relaxation, which were considerable, lasted only for his reign. For, as a natural corollary of the stabilization of the King's income, George III on his accession exchanged the largest fluctuating sources of the hereditary revenue in England and Wales — crown lands, hereditary excise, Post Office — for a fixed annual sum. This sum, which gave George III a Civil List revenue based on the minimum Civil List of George II, £800,000, was considerably lower than George II's income at the end of his reign, and as there was no corresponding reduction in George III's commitments his reign soon produced again the problem of a Civil List debt. A Civil List debt was still regarded as a personal problem for the King, since the Civil List was the 'King's own'. The problem was finally solved, in 1831, by transferring the expenses of civil government from the Civil List, where they could not be adequately controlled, to the Consolidated Fund, where they could be controlled in the same way as army and navy expenses had been controlled since William III's reign. But in George III's reign other expedients were adopted. In 1769, 1777, and 1782 debts on the Civil List were met by parliamentary grant; in 1777 the amount of the Civil List was raised to £900,000 ; in 1782 the Commons for the first time invaded the 'King's own' by regulating the Civil List. The Commons' division of Civil List expenditure into classes, and definition of the order of their payment, was not successful in reducing expenses, and indeed it was fortunate that this was so, for success would not only have delayed the final separation of public from private expenditure but would, immediately, have shattered the financial balance between King and Commons. As it was, the balance was unsettled but not destroyed in 1782, and though afterwards the Commons were presented with a list of Civil List expenses, they did not effectively control these expenses. A Civil List debt was incurred again in 1784, in 1786, and several times in the early nineteenth century, though it was calculated that the debt was never as large as the surplus which George III would have enjoyed had he not surrendered the revenues from the crown lands in 1760.

Only in George II's reign, therefore, had it been in theory possible for the King to disturb the financial balance between King and Commons, that is, to increase his revenue by saving or by making the sources of his hereditary revenues more productive. In practice, it was never possible : even George II's frugality did not succeed in doing more than achieve, towards the end of his reign, a small surplus on the Civil List, and the great increase in the value of the crown lands in the early nineteenth century came too late to increase the King's income. Moreover, the only loophole through which the King could, at any time after 1660, increase his revenues to any appreciable extent without recourse to parliament — borrowing — was not open to any of the Hanoverians. This loophole was closed in William III's reign : the establishment of the system authorizing the King to borrow up to fixed amounts on the security of taxes granted by parliament, the foundation of the Bank of England, which was forbidden to lend to the King without parliamentary sanction, and the beginning of the National Debt, subjected the King's borrowing to parliamentary control, and, by way of compensation for the loss of freedom involved, made it easier for him to borrow by providing a parliamentary guarantee for his loans.

CHAPTER IV

CONNECTIONS BETWEEN KING AND COMMONS, 1716–1832

(i) TIME AND THEORY

ONE of the most obvious modern connections between the House of Commons and the King's ministers is that of time. They normally begin and end life together: a general election is the immediate prelude to the formation of a cabinet which is determined by the result of the election, for the election designates a prime minister and he chooses his colleagues from among the chief members of the party which has obtained a majority at the election. This time-connection did not become normal until after the second Reform Act. Between 1716 and 1783 neither this nor any other time-connection existed: the choice of ministers by the King, and of the House of Commons by the electorate, remained (as of course they were before 1716) separate events, taking place at different times. In theory they were not connected at all; in practice they were connected only in so far as the King and the ministers he had chosen were able to influence the result of the next general election. This ensured that a general election benefited the ministers under whose auspices it was held, but it did not ensure that the House elected remained favourable to those ministers; if it did not, then the King might change some of his ministers to suit the House of Commons, but he would not normally change the House to suit his ministers. Inevit-.ably, therefore, ministers depended for their strength less on general elections than on their ability to retain the favour of the House of Commons before and after general elections. Their dependence in this respect was greater because, after 1716, the House of Commons possessed a great advantage that ministers did not — the advantage of normally lasting for reasonably long and regular periods. While the House of Commons was sometimes strong enough to obtain the dismissal of ministers it disliked, ministers were not strong enough to obtain the dissolution of a parliament they disliked. So, while between 1716 and 1783 general elections took place with some regularity,[1] the length of administrations varied greatly and neither their beginning nor their end coincided with a general election. There were, in this period, three long administrations — Walpole was First Lord of the Treasury for twenty-one years (1721–42), Pelham for eight years (1746–1754), North for twelve (1770–82). On the other hand, the average life of the other fifteen First Lords of the same period was less than eighteen months.

Pitt's long administration (1783–1801) was different. It began a period when, although the Commons still insisted that the Septennial convention was a part of the constitution, as indeed they did until the middle of the nineteenth century, the King often infringed the convention that 'the natural life of Parliaments' was seven years. Indeed, of the thirteen parliaments of the period 1784–1832, only two — that of May 1784 to June 1790 and that of April 1820 to June 1826 — lasted for as long as six years. Three of the eleven premature general elections of these years — those of May 1796, June 1802, and June 1818 — followed dissolutions of parliaments which had been in existence for more than five and a half years: their purpose was to improve the position of the existing ministers in the House of Commons, but they were not

---

[1] All the eleven parliaments which sat between 1716 and 1783 lasted between six and seven years, except that dissolved in August 1727 after the death of George I, and those dissolved in June 1747 and in September 1780, which lasted for six years and five years ten months respectively.

connected with a change of administration, and they could, therefore, appeal for precedent to the general elections of 1747, 1774, and 1780. Two of the others — those of February 1820 and July 1830 — followed the death of a monarch and were therefore only accidentally premature, one — that of April 1831 — preceded the Reform Bill, and one — that of December 1832 — followed it. The remaining four — those of March 1784, October 1806, April 1807, September 1812 — closely followed on changes of administration and were designed to improve the position of a new administration in the Commons. For this there was no precedent. To dissolve a parliament, irrespective of its age, as a postcript to a change of ministers, and in order to provide a new government with a new and favourable House of Commons, is perhaps, from the King's point of view, only a natural corollary of the fact that, in the period 1716 to 1783, the King's influence always enabled his ministers to 'win' general elections. The corollary was, however, acted upon not in this period but in the period of declining influence which followed it, when the 'winning' of general elections by the existing ministers was growing steadily less certain and less easy. For this reason, the most successful of these four general elections was the first, that of March 1784, which was held three months after the formation of Pitt's ministry in order to replace a hostile House of Commons by a more favourable one. This it did so successfully that it is now usually regarded as an election 'of the old kind', won primarily because of the sufficiency and skilful use of the King's patronage. The premature general elections held later in the period, and held more readily because of the 1784 precedent, were less successful. The three dissolutions associated with a change of administration — those of October 1806, April 1807, September 1812 — did improve the position of the new ministers, but the extent of the improvement was in each case in marked contrast with the

immense improvement in 1784. The dissolution of July
1830, which was premature only because of the death of
George IV, resulted in an unexpected and unprecedented
defeat for the government, Wellington's, at the outset of
a new reign, and shortly after the opening of the new
parliament the hostility of the new Commons led Wellington to resign. His resignation was a dangerous precedent
for a new kind of time-connection between Commons and
King's ministers, under which a general election should be
not a postscript but a prelude and cause of a change of
ministers. The unsuccessful premature general election
of January 1835, which followed the dissolution of the first
parliament elected under the Reform Act, and that of June
1841, which followed the disastrous dissolution of the first
parliament of Victoria's reign, proved that after the Reform
Act the King could not lightly use what Brougham described as 'by far the most eminent of the Royal prerogatives' — dissolution — since dissolution could no longer
be relied on to produce for ministers of the King's choice,
whether new in office, as in 1834, or old in office, as in 1841,
a House of Commons strong in their support. Victoria had
learnt this by 1846, when she told Lord John Russell that
dissolution, 'a most valuable and powerful instrument in
the hands of the Crown', ought to be used only exception-
ally and if there was no doubt of the issue, since to dissolve
'and be defeated is a thing most lowering to the Crown and
hurtful to the country'. But the experience of the years
between 1784 and 1832 shows that the value of the instrument had been declining, in inverse proportion to the
frequency of its use, for forty years before the Reform Act.
The fact that this was so did not affect the Commons'
view that every premature dissolution, except in time of real
emergency, dealt a 'death-blow' to the constitution, since
it curtailed their natural life and therefore infringed their
independence. The dissolutions of 1796, 1802, and 1818,
which did not follow changes of ministry, were disliked

because they deprived the Commons of the life which they had come to regard as theirs by right; the dissolutions of 1784, 1806, 1807, and 1812, which did follow changes of ministry, were criticized as abuses of the royal prerogative.[1] On all four occasions it was contended that the duty of ministers who found themselves unable to get on with the House of Commons was to resign. Dissolution in aid of such ministers, so that, in Burke's words, 'parliament should be new modelled until it is fitted to their purposes', was not a legitimate alternative, and ministers who suggested it gave unconstitutional advice to their King. Their advice was particularly reprehensible when, as in 1784, the ministers whom the King dismissed had enjoyed the confidence of the old House of Commons, while the ministers for whom the House was changed had been defeated in the old House. In 1784 it seemed to Burke that a parliament was, without justification, 'sentenced, condemned and executed', and that its dissolution was part of a 'settled plan to destroy, not the form, but the essence of the House of Commons'. By appealing to the people, and even suggesting to them that the King had changed his ministers and dissolved parliament 'in order to rescue the people and their rights out of the hands of the house of commons', the King's advisers had encouraged him in a step which took away the independence of the House of Commons and reduced it to 'a mere appendage of administration'.

At the opening of parliament in December 1806 Lord Hawkesbury, in the House of Lords, while recognizing the King's right to dissolve parliament 'in its fullest extent and plenitude', condemned the late 'unexpected and premature dissolution' of a parliament which had sat only for four sessions, instead of 'submitting to the existing parliament the whole grounds of the negotiation (for

[1] A typical example of contemporary criticism of infringement of the Septennial convention is found in the *Annual Register* for 1806. See Appendix G.

peace)'. In reply Grenville maintained that the failure of negotiations for peace amply justified the King's decision 'to appeal to the sense of his people, to refer to them the conduct of his servants, and thereby to call on them to pronounce, in the eyes of the world, their sense as to the farther prosecution of the contest'. He made no rejoinder to Hawkesbury's suggestion that an extraordinary appeal to the people was an extra-constitutional appeal. In the House of Commons, Canning went so far as to propose an alternative Address in reply to the Speech from the Throne, including in it an expression of 'concern and disapprobation upon the circumstances of surprise and deception which attended the sudden exercise of that prerogative in the dissolution of the late parliament'. His proposal was negatived. At the beginning of parliament in June 1807 an amendment to the Address was moved, both in the Commons and in the Lords, that 'the dissolution of the late parliament, advised by his majesty's ministers, at a time when there existed no difference between any of the branches of the legislature, and no sufficient cause for a fresh appeal to his majesty's people, was justified by no public necessity or advantage'. In the Commons the amendment was defeated by 350 votes to 155 ; in the Lords it was defeated by 160 votes to 67. The dissolution of September 1812 met with similar criticism. It too was clearly designed to strengthen ministers recently appointed. By this time, indeed, premature dissolution had so often followed the Commons' criticism of ministers that the Duke of Northumberland, for example, thought the Regent would have been well advised 'to have determined at once', on the death of Perceval in May, 'to keep in the late Ministers, and dissolve the Parliament'. Again, although, as the *Annual Register* remarked, no recent parliaments 'had been suffered to live out their assigned period', the sudden dissolution occasioned 'general surprise', and was criticized on the grounds that 'no public reason' was given for it and that 'the present parliament had nineteen months to run before its legal expiration'. After conjecturing that the dissolution was, like its two predecessors, connected with disagreements on the question of Catholic emancipation, the *Annual Register* pointed the constitutional moral that, whatever the immediate purpose of ministers in advising dissolution, 'it certainly displayed a confidence in their popularity with the nation at large, or, at least, in the powers in their hands for procuring such a return of representatives as would rather augment than diminish their influence'. The *Edinburgh Review* had, in 1810, pointed the same moral more emphatically, condemning the 'frequent exercise' of the prerogative of dissolution as 'one of the worst kinds of Crown influence — the influence derived from an occasional alliance but very natural between the mob and arbitrary power'.

The House of Commons and the King's ministers, then, were not normally connected in time in the period 1716–1832, though in the last fifty years of this period the House of Commons was sometimes dissolved as an aftermath of a change of ministry. Moreover, the fact that the lives of ministers and Commons did not coincide was perhaps the greatest practical safeguard of the theoretical independence of King and Commons. The most accurate as well as the most popular theory of the eighteenth-century constitution was that the tripartite division of the supreme legislative power between strong and independent bodies, each of which had its own function, and was if necessary checked and balanced by the others, secured liberty and prevented tyranny. This theory was well developed before Montesquieu's visit to England in 1729, and it can hardly be said that the *Esprit des Lois* added anything to it. Montésquieu's conception of a parliamentary balance of power between King, Lords, and Commons is indeed unexceptionable. But his idea that the English constitution illustrated his contention that the degree of civil liberty in a state depended on the degree of separation of the functions of government — legislative, executive, and judicial — is easily refuted.[1] The two theories are not of course necessarily related — indeed they are not easily compatible — and for most people the first was the essence of the constitution and an adequate description of it. John Toland, for example, in 1716 wrote of 'our three Estates of King, Lords and Commons, making up the supreme Legislative power of the nation . . . with the judicious distribution of the privileges and prerogatives peculiar to each Estate; and how that as they are mutual checks and awes on one another, so they are to one another mutual lights and assistants. In the equilibrium of this body, and the unanimity of their deliberations, consists our greatest happiness; while, to our further comfort, the nature of their proceedings is such, that none of the Estates can scarce ever be surprised or seduced into any pernicious measures, but that the other two may seasonably interpose.'

Nor are the two trios — King, Lords, and Commons; executive, legislature, judicature — identical. Indeed, Montesquieu clearly did not consider them identical, nor did he attempt to find a relation between them. In fact,

---

[1] In March 1806 Montesquieu's authority as an interpreter of the English constitution was repudiated, in both Houses, in the course of debates on resolutions deploring the inclusion in the cabinet of Ellenborough, Lord Chief Justice. In the House of Lords, St. John contended that the 'blended' composition and functions of the Lords 'served to prove how little, relative to the constitution of this country, could be gathered from Montesquieu. He should look to better sources . . . the Statute Book, and the practice and usage of the country', while Hawkesbury 'would not look to any foreign writer for the principles of the British constitution' (*Parliamentary History*, vi. 261, 275). In the Commons, Bond maintained that the theory of separation of powers 'was very ingenious, but it did not practically apply to the circumstances and constitution of this country', and Fox declared that, for Montesquieu 'as a general political philosopher, I entertain the highest respect; but the application of his principles to, or his clear comprehension of, the constitution of England, I am not disposed to admit' (*ibid.* 295, 313). In the Lords the resolution was negatived without a division; in the Commons it was defeated by 222 to 64.

therefore, Montesquieu offered two separate analyses of the constitution : for him the balance between King, Lords, and Commons signified a balance between the three estates of the realm, representing the three 'pure' types of government — monarchy, aristocracy, democracy — rather than between the three branches of the supreme legislature. On the other hand, the separation of executive, legislature, and judicature represented a division between the three functions of government. It is, however, possible to relate the two trios. Those who did so saw that mixture, not separation, was the essential characteristic of the functions of government, and that, as both King and Lords derived much of their power from outside parliament, so the Commons, by a sort of compensatory principle, had the greatest power in parliament. Blackstone, for example, considered that it was 'highly necessary for preserving the balance of the constitution, that the executive power should be a branch, though not the whole, of the legislature.   The total union of them, we have seen, would be productive of tyranny ; the total disjunction of them, for the present, would in the end produce the same effects, by causing that union against which it seems to provide. . . . To hinder therefore any such encroachment (of the two Houses) the king is himself a part of the parliament ; and, as this is the reason for his being so, very properly the share of legislation which the constitution has placed in the crown, consists in the power of rejecting, rather than resolving.' An attempt to relate the two trios more closely was made by the author of *The Constitution*, written in 1781 in opposition to Burke's plan of reform. 'Is there not', the author wrote, 'a three-fold division of the legislative power well understood and agreed to by the three branches of the legislature ? The commons are in sole possession of all money-grants *in*, but not *out* of parliament : the ulti-mate court of judicature, over the whole property of the Kingdom, is exclusively appropriated to the lords. Lastly, the *executive* power to GOVERN, is exclusively vested in the King.'

For most people, however, the first theory — that of parliamentary balance — was the fundamental principle of the constitution, and this was so because parliament was the supreme, if not the sovereign, power in the constitution. The parliamentary balance between King, Lords, and Commons was generally thought to be preserved by self-interest : if any one of the three tried to increase its power the other two would 'reduce the offending power within its proper bounds'. The revolution of 1689 was itself the outstanding practical illustration, as it was the guarantee, of this principle. Edward Wortley Montagu, writing in 1759, was only one of many who pointed out that at 'the late happy revolution' Lords and Commons had '*recourse* to the joint exercise of the restraining power, which is the inherent *ressource* of all mixed Governments'. Montagu was also representative of general opinion in insisting that the chief glory of the revolution was that Lords and Commons had exercised their 'joint coercive power' in a moderate and patriotic way : they had restrained a King without either abolishing Kingship or reducing it to impotence. This view, that the value of the balance lay in preserving all three powers, and not only in preventing the aggression of any one of them, was indeed so general that, in de Lolme's opinion, the practical working of the balance meant primarily that Lords and Commons 'have by turns effectually defeated the attacks of each other upon the King's prerogatives'. De Lolme gave examples of occasions on which this had happened : the Commons, on the one hand, in 1693 rejected a Bill for annual sessions, and in 1719 successfully resisted the Peerage Bill, an attempt by the Lords 'to wrest from the Crown a prerogative which is one of its finest flowers ; and is, besides, the only check it has on the dangerous views which that House (which may stop both money-bills and all other bills) might be brought to entertain'; the Lords, on the other hand, successfully challenged the Commons' practice of tacking non-financial measures on to money Bills, they rejected the second Exclusion Bill in 1680, they constantly rejected Place Bills. Even more important than the preservation of the parliamentary balance by securing the defeat of open attacks on the powers of the crown was, de Lolme thought, the stability which resulted from the tendency for the 'mutual jealousy of Lords and Commons to prevent even the making of such attacks'. 'The views of each of those two Houses', he wrote, 'destroying upon those occasions, the opposite views of the other; like those positive and negative quantities (if I am allowed the expression) which destroy each other on the opposite sides of an equation.'

The very accuracy of the theory of parliamentary balance to some extent invalidates the theory of separation of powers. For, while the King did act as a check on the Lords and Commons in parliament, he was enabled to check them less because he was a part of parliament than because he was head of the executive. Equally, while the Commons could, with the co-operation of the Lords, impeach the King's ministers, and could, without the Lords, threaten to refuse supplies, their motive was, in both cases, less that the King was a part of parliament than that he was the executive intruding into parliament. Indeed, criticism of the theory of parliamentary balance usually alleges not that it is inaccurate but that it is incomplete: it lays more stress on checks and balances than on the co-operation which is necessary if balance and mixed government is to work.

Yet the theory of balance does not assume, as some of its critics have implied, continual conflict of the balanced powers, but rather, as de Lolme suggested, a general and normal harmony between them, and, in the last resort, security against tyranny. 'The balance of the constitution', remarked the *Annual Register* in 1807, 'is only a metaphor : were it, strictly speaking, a balance among opposite powers, government would be at a dead stand, when the counterpoise should be most exact and perfect. The impulsion, the soul, the *spiritus rector* of the British government, depends on the harmonious understanding and co-operation of all its members.' The basis for this co-operation, in the relation between King and Commons, was the distribution of the King's patronage in such a way as to ensure that every House of Commons contained a body of placemen who were normally disposed, but never bound, to support the government of the day. This body was at no time large enough, nor was it docile enough, either to reduce the Commons to subservience or to elevate the King to independence. Nevertheless, it was large enough, at least in the period of balance between 1716 and 1783, to provide a vital link between a House of Commons chosen by the electorate and ministers chosen by the King. It is true that this method of facilitating co-operation between King and Commons was not acclaimed, or even discussed, by all those who praised the parliamentary balance of power. It was, for example, not acclaimed by Blackstone. For the crown influence which Blackstone described was mainly extra-parliamentary : it consisted of the patronage created by the increase in taxation and the national debt since 1689, that is, the generally disliked revenue officers. Again, Blackstone unhesitatingly preferred 'the milder voice of influence' to 'the stern commands of prerogative', but this did not prevent him from looking forward to the day when 'this adventitious power of the Crown will slowly and imperceptibly diminish, as it slowly and imperceptibly rose'. This was certainly to ignore the value of the parliamentary function of patronage. On the other hand, it may fairly be argued that Blackstone's purpose, to examine the laws of England, did not require him to consider a method of achieving co-operation between King and Commons which depended mainly not on law but on convention. There were others — de Lolme, for example — who did not praise the method by which co-operation between King and Commons was achieved. This was partly because their interest lay primarily in the principles rather than in the practice of the constitution, and partly because balance did not, for them, imply lack of co-operation. For it was the principles of the constitution — checks, balances, mixture — which ensured liberty and provided safeguards against tyranny. These principles could be and, it was believed, were secured by the operation of law; practice had to be left to the operation of convention, and convention was, after all, only the superstructure of the constitution.

It is, however, not difficult to find contemporaries who, because they were interested in the working of the constitution rather than its legal foundation, took notice of the superstructure. These men did not ignore the parliamentary function of patronage, nor did they regard it, as some critics of the theory of parliamentary balance have done, as a system which was separate from, or even cut across, the balance of the constitution. On the contrary, they considered that patronage was an essential part of the balance of the constitution, and that it had become so after 1689. To Hume, in 1742, the existence of the influence 'which arises from the offices and honours which are at the disposal of the Crown' was the main reason why the Commons did not escape from the parliamentary balance, and the gravest constitutional problem of limited monarchy was to maintain that influence at such a level as will 'form a proper counterbalance to the other parts of the constitution'. Paley, in 1785, urged all groups of parliamentary reformers to pause and reflect 'whether the influence so loudly complained of can be destroyed, or even diminished, without danger to the state'. He reminded them that the period of government by means of the 'more successful expedient of *influence*' had followed a period when 'the King carried his measures in parliament by *intimidation*', and that influence was 'a necessary weight to cast into the scale, to set the balance equal' in view of the 'great share of power' possessed by the House of Commons since 1689. For this reason, Paley insisted, while 'the zeal of some men beholds this influence with jealousy, which nothing but its abolition can appease, many wise and virtuous politicians deem a considerable portion of it to be as necessary a part of the British constitution, as any other ingredient in the composition; to be that, indeed, which gives cohesion and solidity to the whole'. Hume emphatically denied Bolingbroke's contention that 'the dependence of Parliament, in every degree, is an infringement of British liberty', and his denial was quoted with approval in 1780 by the author of *A Letter to Lord North*.[1] The purpose of the *Letter* was to examine the parliamentary function of patronage in order to show that the economical reformers were wrong in thinking 'that the Crown has *too much* influence at its disposal'. Patronage existed, the author wrote, because 'it would be impossible for the executive department of Government to be carried on by a Monarch, who was not at liberty to choose in whom he would place his confidence. . . . It was not originally given for the purpose of creating an influence in the legislature; but that influence was an unavoidable, and, as we have seen, a beneficial consequence of it.' Thus, with Hume, the author insisted that the greatest problem of limited monarchy was 'to ascertain the degree [of influence] which ought to exist', and to ensure that it did exist.

It was, indeed, just because the system of influence was recognized to be a means to an end, that it was praised less generally and less vehemently in the period of balance

[1] *Letter to Lord North on his Re-election into the House of Commons, by a member of the late Parliament.* Bodleian Library, *Godwyn Pamphlets*, vol. 1938. See Appendix F.

than it was when, at the turn of the eighteenth century, it began to work badly and therefore to endanger the end. In the fifty years before the Reform Act the crown was steadily deprived of patronage until its resources were no longer sufficient to manage the House of Commons. It was in this period of decline that influence was most valued in itself, for it then seemed to be not only a piece of machinery but the only possible link between King and Commons and the only guarantee of harmony between them. Accordingly, the decline of influence was feared because it threatened to make government impossible. For the same reason, the wisest of the opponents of the Reform Bill opposed it not because it enfranchised Manchester, or Leeds, but because it reduced the volume of influence still further, at a time when there was urgent need not for less but for more co-operation between King and Commons.

(ii) The Period of Balance, 1716–83

In the period 1716–83, when the Septennial convention ensured to the Commons an existence separate from and independent of the existence of the King's ministers, connection between King and Commons was achieved through the use of influence. Influence was exerted at two stages : during elections, in order to produce a House of Commons favourable to the existing ministers, and later, to assist in the management of a House of Commons which, for part at least of the life of every administration, had been elected under the auspices of a previous one. At both stages the influence available was much smaller than the whole of the King's patronage, for it was limited to the filling up of vacancies as they occurred : vacancies could not normally be created for political reasons, and the number filled by any particular administration depended therefore primarily on how long it lasted.

The direct influence of the King over elections was small : the government only 'won' general elections because, at each of them, the King's influence was supplemented by the much larger influence of the various magnates — usually peers — then supporting the government. The influence of these magnates was strong in the boroughs, weak in the counties. This was partly because the county franchise was uniform, partly because the county electorate was larger and more scattered, partly because of the traditional independence of the country gentry, who formed the core of the electorate. The county members returned to parliament were themselves country gentlemen, usually proud of their independence, not seeking office, and not easily linked with the government. It was because, in Oldfield's words, 'the political integrity (of the counties) is spotless, when compared with the delinquency of the boroughs', that those parliamentary reformers who were concerned to reduce the influence of the peers as well as that of the King, proposed to do so by increasing the number of county members. Chatham, for example, in 1770 advocated an addition to the county representation 'in order to operate as a balance against the weight of the several corrupt and venal boroughs'; the younger Pitt, in May 1783, thought that an addition of not less than one hundred county members, 'gentlemen the least liable to the seduction of corrupt influence, the most deeply interested in the liberty and prosperity of the country', would provide 'an effectual counterbalance to the weight of the boroughs, without being an innovation in the form of the constitution'. Pitt admitted that this would make the House of Commons larger than was desirable. But he hoped that its inflated size might be gradually reduced as a result of the disfranchising of boroughs where it was proved, before a committee appointed under the Grenville Act of 1770, that the majority of electors 'had been bribed and corrupted'. The more radical proposal, then and later, was to reform the House of Commons by exchanging county representation for that of the rotten boroughs : this had the advantage of not increasing the size of the House of Commons, but it had the disadvantage of involving arbitrary disfranchisement. The 'delinquency' of the boroughs was due partly to their small electorates and partly to the great variety and uncertainty of the franchise. Nearly three-quarters of the members of the House of Commons sat for boroughs. Of the 203 English and Welsh boroughs, which, between 1677 and 1822, supplied 417 members, twenty-two had more than 1000 electors and approximately twenty-five had between 500 and 1000. The influence of the peers was greatest in those of the small boroughs where voting depended on landed property : in pocket boroughs, which could be sold outright, and in burgage tenure boroughs, where votes were attached to particular pieces of property, liable to certain feudal services, and could therefore be bought by the agents of peers interested in borough mongering.

The large influence of the peers over borough elections, the fact that at the beginning of George III's reign about a quarter of the members of the Commons were younger sons of peers, and the fact that ministers usually either were or became peers — only two sat in the Commons at the beginning of George III's reign — provided the basis of the influence of the House of Lords over the composition of the House of Commons in the eighteenth century. The nature of this influence was itself a guarantee that the Lords would not, as a body, encroach on the powers of the Commons ; but, on the other hand, the great extent of their influence meant that governments were necessarily based on temporary working alliances between groups of peers, each controlling, to a lesser or greater degree, a group of members of the House of Commons who owed their election wholly or partly to peers. The strength of this group system can be seen, for example,

by the way in which, from Walpole's administration on-
wards, government supporters were invited to attend the
cockpit meetings held on the eve of each parliamentary
session : in the middle of the eighteenth century some
two-thirds of the members invited to hear the reading of
the King's speech were invited not directly but through
the intermediary of a patron in the House of Lords.

By contrast, there were not more than twenty-five or
thirty boroughs where elections were controlled directly
by the government of the day. These, the Treasury,
Admiralty, and Ordnance boroughs, were controlled by
the government in the sense that a majority or at least a
considerable part of the electors held small crown offices
and were expected to vote for government candidates.
The Treasury boroughs, for example, were boroughs with
small electorates and a franchise based on office : it was
in most cases confined to the mayor and corporation, and
perhaps the freemen, most of whom held some local office
under the Boards of Customs and Excise. Even here the
government's control was precarious, for Treasury influence over revenue appointments was never undisputed.
It was at its strongest towards the middle of the eighteenth
century, but by the end of the century the revenue boards
had regained control over their own appointments. The
Treasury's loss of revenue patronage was far more effective
in reducing government influence over borough elections
than Crewe's Act of 1782, which disqualified revenue
officers from voting.

At every general election, the small direct government
influence, added to the large influence of the peers then
supporting the government, usually because they were
members of it or connected with it, produced a House of
Commons in which the majority of members were disposed to support the King's ministers. This indeed was
held to be the proper function of general elections. On the
other hand, the disposition of every new House to support

the existing ministers was never either reliable or lasting, for the idea that formed opposition to the government was factious and unpatriotic was counterweighted by the fact that no government could rely on the support of a formed and fixed party in the House of Commons. Electioneering, though not easy, was from the point of view of the government in office always successful;[1] the government's greater problem was to manage first a House of Commons elected under the auspices of preceding ministers, and, in course of time, the House of Commons elected in its place.

The problem of providing the government of the day with enough support in the Commons to carry on the government depended for its solution primarily on the distribution of crown patronage and the management of the crown placemen in the House. The influence of government peers over the members they had helped to get elected was, of course, a help in the management of the Commons, but this influence was always offset by the similar influence of opposition peers, and was liable to change sides, during the lifetime of a parliament, as the effect of a change of administration. The management of the Commons was for several reasons more difficult than electioneering. The grant of an office was regarded, on both sides, as a reward for services rendered, not as a guarantee of firm support in the future. The beneficiaries of crown patronage in the Commons, the King's friends, were necessarily the prop of all eighteenth-century governments, but the prop was not a firm one, for they were not a political party and they were not united in support of a particular policy. Indeed, as the number of placemen appointed by previous governments

[1] The general election of 1741 came nearer to 'failure' than any other in this period. Even this election, however, did not produce a result decisive enough to be called a 'defeat' for the government. Walpole's defeat in the Commons, in February 1742, on the Chippenham election case was due less to the successes of his opponents at the general election than to later defections of his supporters.

was always larger than those appointed by the existing government, it was desirable that they should not be bound to a specific programme. The fact that they were not so bound, however, made group management impossible : management necessarily consisted in the careful handling, and constant tending, of each individual member of a very miscellaneous group, which could indeed only be regarded as a group in the sense that all its members had, at different times and in different degrees, received a mark of favour from some government.

The size of this group, which was defined in the main by the 1707 Act and the Acts excluding from the House of Commons the officers of the main revenue departments, was restricted in 1742 by the only important Place Act passed after 1716. The Act excluded from the House, without possibility of re-election, lesser civil servants in the main government departments — the Treasury, the Exchequer, the Admiralty, the offices of the Secretaries of State, the offices of the Paymasters of the Army and Navy — and in certain smaller revenue departments ; Commissioners and lesser officers of the Irish Revenue Departments and of the Navy and Victualling Offices ; civil and military employees in Gibraltar and Minorca (except regimental officers). It seems that this exclusion, like earlier Place Acts, did not, in practice, greatly reduce the number of placemen in the House of Commons, though it had a large potential and a small actual influence on their character.

In the middle of the eighteenth century about 200 members of the House of Commons held places of some kind.[1] These members were not equally valuable to the government nor equally consistent in their support of it. Most reliable were those who held active administrative offices, but of these there were less than forty. Rather less than half this group could be classed as ministerial :

[1] Not including contractors, of whom there were between 30 and 40.

two or three ministers — the First Lord of the Treasury or, more often, the Chancellor of the Exchequer, usually one of the Secretaries of State, sometimes the Secretary at War or some other minister; the Law Officers of the Crown; and perhaps a dozen junior ministers — members of the Treasury Board, the Admiralty Board, and the Board of Trade. The remainder of the group of active office-holders, lower in political dignity but in some ways more reliable, consisted of between fifteen and twenty civil servants, who were permanent in office and only half political in their interests. These political civil servants, who formed the nucleus of the King's friends, were the most stable element in eighteenth-century parliaments, and as many of them sat for Treasury and Admiralty boroughs they seemed almost permanent in the House of Commons as well as in office. Apart from the active group of ministers and civil servants, about 160 members of the House held places of more or less importance. They formed a very miscellaneous group, connected with the government not because they were a part of the executive but only because, at some time, they had received a favour from it or from one of its predecessors. The group was composed, in the middle of the century, of, approximately, 50 court and household officials, 45 holders of sinecures, 10 pensioners, 60 army and navy officers. It was these men, who had little in common and were much less reliable than the 'professional' group of working placemen, who required constant management, care, and attention, for it was they who formed the potential numerical support for the government in the House of Commons. The difficulties of management were increased by the fact that, at any one time, most of the members of this group had been appointed not by the existing ministers but by their predecessors.

All the members of the large second group of placemen,[1] and all except a dozen of the first, were subject to

---

[1] Except army and navy officers accepting a new commission.

the requirement, imposed by the Succession to the Crown Act of 1707, of vacation of seat and re-election on appointment to office. This requirement did not in practice exclude many placemen from the Commons,[1] but it had a considerable effect on the distribution of places, and an examination of the number and kind of placemen re-elected throws considerable light on the problems of management which faced ministers.

In the eleven parliaments of the period 1716–83, 829 members of parliament were appointed to places, and of these 658 were re-elected. The proportion of placemen re-elected, about four-fifths of those appointed, remained fairly constant, though the actual number re-elected varied from 32 in the 1747–54 parliament to 102 in the 1761–8 parliament. Over the whole period, the average number of placemen who sat in the House was something like 200. In all eleven parliaments, therefore, an average of about 70 per cent of the placemen in the House of Commons did not owe their appointment to the King's existing ministers and were therefore not disposed by motives of personal gratitude or sympathy to support them. That they were, nevertheless, generally disposed, though they were not bound, to give a general support to ministers who had not appointed them reflected a feeling of loyalty to the King, whose servants they were, rather than to any particular set of his ministers. This feeling was more like an impersonal civil service loyalty than political loyalty.

The vast majority of placemen of the second group, and about a half of the first group, did not change with the administration, but by-elections due to acceptance of office were, of course, more numerous in those parliaments

---

[1] About one-fifth of the placemen appointed in the parliaments of the period 1716–83 were not re-elected : this represents an average of about 7 per cent of the total number of placemen in the House. Not all of these were rejected by their constituents : in some parliaments nearly half of those appointed were ineligible for re-election and a few did not seek re-election.

which saw several changes of administration than in those which saw none or only one.[1]   In the parliaments of 1741–7 and 1780–4, for example, which saw four changes of administration, there were respectively 71 and 75 re-elections, while in the parliaments of 1734–41 and 1774–80, which saw no changes of administration, there were respectively 39 and 38 re-elections.   There were changes of administration during the course of six of the eleven parliaments of the period 1716–83.   It was only in these six parliaments that the placemen who were re-elected included not only an arbitrary number of officials, mostly non-political, appointed to replace those who died or retired, but also the officials appointed and re-elected when the administration changed.   Most of these officials were junior ministers or civil servants, and, for the first few months of any administration, they were the only placemen appointed by it and therefore the only ones who had any reason to be in sympathy with it.   Although their number increased during the period 1716–83, there were never many of them.   There were, for example, only two appointments and re-elections, both ministers, in the first three months of Walpole's administration, seven in the first three months of Pelham's and North's, fifteen at the beginning of Pitt's.[2]   One reason why the number was small was that junior ministers and civil servants did not all sit in the Commons, and, like ministers, were not all changed when an administration changed.   Of the seven re-elections at the beginning of North's administration, one was a minister — North himself — three were junior ministers, one was a Household officer, and two were civil servants; of the fifteen re-elections at the beginning of Pitt's administration two were ministers, one was a law officer, ten were junior ministers, and two were civil servants.

No new administration wished its supporters to be defeated in by-elections following their appointment to

[1] See Appendix B.   [2] See Appendix D.

office, and there was an evident tendency for junior ministerial appointments to be made from members for safe boroughs and not from members for counties or for boroughs with a wide franchise. On the other hand, every new administration found that some of the safest boroughs of all — Treasury and Admiralty boroughs, Cinque ports, Cornish boroughs — were not available for ministerial appointments, for they were already occupied by other placemen, often civil servants or household officers, most of whom did not change with the administration. The tendency was therefore necessarily less marked at the beginning of an administration than later in its existence, when safe borough seats became vacant. Nevertheless, few of the placemen appointed at the beginning of the administrations of the period 1716–83 failed to secure re-election.

The number of non-ministerial placemen appointed and re-elected by the administrations of the period 1716–83 varied a good deal, and so did the kind of placemen re-elected. The variation was due not to political reasons but, primarily, to variations in the length of administrations, for there were only places of this kind to be filled if they became vacant by death or retirement. A government was therefore only able to appoint members of parliament to those places which fell vacant either between its own appointment and the dissolution of parliament, or between the beginning of a parliament and the end of its own tenure of office, or during the whole parliament in the few cases when a government was fortunate enough to live longer than a parliament. The total number of placemen re-elected during North's administration, for example, was only 83 : 38 between North's appointment as First Lord of the Treasury in January 1770 and the dissolution of parliament in September 1774 : 38 in the parliament of 1774–80 ; 7 between the beginning of the parliament of 1780–4 and North's resignation in March 1782.[1] Of

[1] See Appendix C.

this total about 50 belonged to the ministerial and civil service group. In the same period, 1770–82, 30 placemen were reappointed and not re-elected, more than half of them because their places made them ineligible. In each of the three parliaments there was a total of 170 or 180 placemen, including about 50 army and navy officers. Few administrations lasted as long as North's, and it is clear that the number of placemen appointed by most governments formed a much smaller proportion of the total number of placemen in the House.

These two facts — the small number of placemen which any administration could appoint in its first few months of office, and the small number, compared with the total number of placemen in the Commons, which an administration could ever appoint — explain why the volume of patronage was so much smaller than it looked, why the appointment of placemen was only a small part of the task of managing the House of Commons, and why 'constant care and attention' were needed in order to persuade placemen to support the King's ministers.

The task of managing the King's friends in the House of Commons naturally fell to those of his ministers who, as his agents, were responsible for the distribution of crown patronage. These ministers were not all of equal importance. The chief reason for the ascendancy of the First Lord of the Treasury both in the cabinet and in the Commons was that his office gave him the duty of distributing a larger part of the total crown patronage than any other minister, and this made him chief manager of the Commons. Much of this Treasury patronage consisted of local offices in the revenue departments. The fact that these offices were not tenable with seats in the Commons did not prevent their being distributed to friends and supporters of particular members of parliament, with the object of keeping the support of those members: indeed, local revenue offices and local postmasterships were often regarded, by the electorate as well as by members of parliament, as the 'property' of the member in whose constituency they were. There were other reasons for the ascendancy of the First Lord : after the beginning of the eighteenth century, when the other Treasury Lords had sunk to a secondary place and the Commissioners of Customs and Excise were debarred from membership of the Commons, he assumed sole responsibility for financial policy, and this was peculiarly the concern of the Commons. The First Lord's association with the Commons was, moreover, unlike that of other ministers, continuous, for if he was not himself a member of the Commons he was provided with a deputy there, the Chancellor of the Exchequer. The office of Chancellor of the Exchequer remained a secondary one : if the First Lord was a commoner he held the office himself, so that its chief value was to give the First Lord, if necessary, a deputy in the Commons. This position was not altered until Peel's ministry of 1841–6, when Peel appointed a separate Chancellor of the Exchequer and both First Lord and Chancellor of the Exchequer sat in the Commons.[1]

Although the office of Chancellor of the Exchequer provided the First Lord of the Treasury with an adequate deputy for financial matters, his second function, the management of the Commons, was not so easily performed when he was not himself in the House. The First Lords in the four long administrations of the eighteenth century — Walpole, Pelham, North, the younger Pitt — all sat in the Commons, but the thirteen First Lords who, between Walpole and Pitt, were peers, had an average life

---

[1] In November 1778 North proposed that he should remain 'in the Commons as First Lord of the Treasury' and give up the office of Chancellor of the Exchequer to Charles Jenkinson. But North did not think that this could be a permanent arrangement 'because, although the Public Affairs would be greatly benefited by it, Lord North would, in a short time become a cipher at his Board'. The proposal was, in fact, intended as a half-way house to North's resignation after one more session, and George III rejected it outright. (See *Correspondence of George III,* iv. 216-17.)

in office of less than eighteen months. There were, of course, personal reasons for the brevity and weakness of administrations led by First Lords who were not in the House of Commons, but beneath the personal reasons there lurked the constant factor of the difficulty of managing the Commons from the House of Lords. For the management of the Commons was facilitated by the distribution of patronage but never depended on this alone : it depended also on personal leadership, and, for this reason, the practice of having a deputy in the House of Commons never worked as well with this side of the functions of the First Lord as it did with the financial side. Newcastle's difficulties after the death of Pelham in March 1754, and many of the difficulties which faced the leaders of the six short administrations of the first ten years of George III's reign, were due either to the fact that the deputies left in the Commons were unreliable or to the fact that their leadership of the House was disputed by a more outstanding member, usually Pitt, who harassed every ministry he did not join and was seldom willing to co-operate with the other members of those he did join. When, in 1766, Pitt accepted a peerage and tried to manage the Commons from the House of Lords, he was himself faced with opposition from an unreliable deputy in the Commons — Charles Townshend, Chancellor of the Exchequer.

Yet the advantages of having a ministry composed mainly of peers, who, for the purposes of managing the Commons, added their own influence to that of the government, were in general considered to outweigh the advantages of having the House of Commons managed by a commoner, both in the period 1716–83 and in the period 1784–1832. Indeed, it seems that the problem of managing the Commons from the Lords, as distinct from the general problem of managing the Commons, was more acute in the earlier than in the later period. For the developments which promised some compensation for the decline of patronage — greater cabinet solidarity, the tighter control of the prime minister over other members of the cabinet, and the consequent greater reliability of deputies in the Commons — clearly also made it easier for the First Lord to manage the Commons even if he was not there in person to lead it. None of these developments had gone far by 1832, but their effect on the problem of management from the Lords can already be seen in the nature of Liverpool's relations with the members of his administration and with the Commons. Their effect became more pronounced later in the nineteenth century, and was reinforced by the growth of party discipline. So, while Canning in the early nineteenth century and Wellington in the 1820s both thought it desirable that the prime minister should himself lead the Commons, Gladstone in 1868 saw no reason why the prime minister should not be in the House of Lords.

(iii) THE PERIOD OF DECLINE, 1784–1832

In the period between 1784 and 1832 a relentless process of reducing the volume of the King's influence undermined the connections between King and Commons, and consequently weakened co-operation between them, to such an extent that the complete triumph of the Commons, held in check by the conventions of the period of balance, seemed about to be achieved. Yet this triumph would have been an unintentional achievement, for the King's influence was, almost entirely, reduced not as a result of political assaults by the Commons in the interests of their own independence, but as a result of administrative reforms undertaken, largely on the initiative of the King's ministers, in the interests of efficiency : not, that is, by excluding placemen from the House of Commons but by abolishing places.

The political assaults of the Commons — attempts to exclude placemen from the House either by general Place Bills or, later, by Place Bills excluding particular kinds of placemen; attempts to forbid placemen from influencing elections and even to deprive placemen of the right to vote — were in the main confined to the period of balance before 1783. The attempts had some success; but their aim, the reduction of influence, was not realized. The exclusion of revenue officers from the Commons did not seriously diminish the political value of revenue patronage, since its distribution to non-members, for political reasons, was not restricted. Moreover, neither the exclusion of revenue officers and of other placemen, nor the imposing of the requirement of re-election on members accepting nearly all offices, seriously reduced the number of place-men in the House. Ineffectiveness is the keynote not only of the Place Acts of the first half of the eighteenth century but also of the last serious attack on the King's influence, the Economical Reform movement of the early 1780s. The movement was spectacular because of Burke's championship and Dunning's Resolutions, and it thrived on growing discontent with the conduct of the American war, but its achievement was small, and the three Acts passed in 1782, when the Rockingham group was in office, did not effect a considerable reduction of crown patronage. It was very greatly reduced, however, in the next fifty years, as a result of administrative reforms carried out by men who were interested not in curtailing the King's influence, nor in destroying the link between King and Commons, but in securing 'a better regulation of business'.

The process of administrative reform began in the 1780s with two great government enquiries — one into the methods and organization of the government departments concerned with collecting and spending revenue, the other into the numbers, duties, and payment of the public servants in the chief government departments — and

ended with the Commons' last enquiry into sinecures in
1834. The appointment in 1780 of Commissioners to
'examine . . . the public Accounts of the Kingdom' was
North's answer to pressure from the economical reformers.
It was not, however, the answer they wanted : they attacked
the Commissioners because none of them was a member of
parliament. The Commissioners appointed in 1785 to
enquire into the 'Fees, Gratuities, Perquisites and Emolu-
ments . . . received in the . . . Public Offices' were
appointed on Pitt's initiative and not because of pressure
from an opposition. The methods of securing a 'better
regulation of business' recommended in the fifteen Reports
of the first Commission, and the ten Reports of the second,
involved the reorganization of many government departments ; the abolition of sinecures and the beginning of a
regular system of superannuation for civil servants ; payment by salary only instead of by salary and fees, and out
of public money instead of from the Civil List ; appointments on grounds of suitability instead of favour ; the
elimination of political interest from the grant of government loans and contracts and from leases of crown lands.
These administrative reforms were all started, and some
of them were completed, before 1832. Their political
result was a very large reduction both in the volume of
patronage and in the volume of what George Rose, Pitt's
Secretary to the Treasury, called the 'imperceptible influence' at the disposal of the government for political
use.

The visible effect of administrative reform on the
composition of the House of Commons was a great reduction of the number of placemen who sat there. This was
a reduction which Place Acts had not brought about. It
affected not the first group of ministers and working placemen but only the large miscellaneous second group of
government beneficiaries. Indeed, the size of the first
group rose from nearly 40 in the middle of the eighteenth

century to nearly 50 in 1780, and between 50 and 55 in the early nineteenth century. But the size of the second group fell from about 160 in the middle of the eighteenth century to about 60 in the early nineteenth century.[1] All sections of the second group shared in the decline: by 1808, for example, the number of Household and Court officials in the Commons, which was about 50 in the middle of the eighteenth century, had fallen to about 10, and in the same period the number of sinecurists fell from about 45 to about 20, and the number of army and navy officers from about 60 to about 30. The shrinkage continued, less rapidly, in the next twenty years: by 1830 the number of non-working placemen in the House of Commons (excluding army and navy officers) had fallen to about 20.

This reduction, large as it was, was only the parliamentary reflection of the general shrinkage in the period 1784–1832 in the volume of government patronage available for distribution 'for purely political reasons'. For most of this patronage had always, in the period 1716–1783, been distributed not to members of parliament but to non-members, in the hope of obtaining their votes, retaining their support or pleasing their members. This non-parliamentary patronage was also drastically reduced. For example, between 1782 and 1800, 1100 offices in the revenue departments, none of them tenable by members of parliament, were condemned as sinecures or semi-sinecures and either abolished or merged with 'working' offices, and the Select Committee on Sinecures of 1834 found, in the whole public service, only 55 sinecures, some of which had already been condemned to abolition on the death of their holders. Moreover, one of the largest contributions to the shrinkage in revenue patronage came

[1] The Union with Ireland added about 20 placemen to the House of Commons. The 3rd Report of the Committee on National Expenditure, 1808, lists 47 English, 4 Scottish, and 15 Irish placemen, and 18 legal officers (*Parliamentary Papers*, 1808, iii. (331), Appendix 80). Of the total of 84, more than 50 belonged to the first group of active office-holders.

not from its abolition but from its transfer. Treasury control over revenue patronage, which reached its peak towards the middle of the eighteenth century, had never been accepted without protest by the revenue boards, and by 1815 the revenue commissioners had succeeded, in the name of administrative efficiency, in securing most of it for themselves. The commissioners were not politicians, they were themselves excluded from parliament, and they were undoubtedly less vulnerable to political pressure than the Treasury was. The transfer of revenue patronage to the revenue boards was one of the chief reasons why the Treasury was short of patronage in the early nineteenth century.

The frequent complaints about the dearth of patronage in the early nineteenth century leave no doubt that ministers responsible for carrying on the King's government ascribed their difficulties to the fact that the patronage left to the King was no longer adequate for the purpose of linking King and Commons. Even the younger Pitt had been accused of having destroyed so many places that he was forced to bestow peerages on the supporters of his government, so removing them from the Commons and weakening his friends there. Pitt's difficulties were, however, certainly less acute than those of his successors. Lord Hawkesbury, in 1800, stated in the House of Commons that, as a result of the 'spirit of internal reform' which had prevailed since 1782, the number of members of the House of Commons holding places under the government (including contractors) had fallen from 118 in 1778 to 52 in 1800, 'so that, within these twenty years, there has been a diminution of the influence of the Crown, in this House, arising from places and contracts, of more than one-half'.[1] Charles Arbuthnot, Secretary to the

---

[1] It is not always easy to reconcile or compare figures given by contemporaries for the number of placemen in the Commons at different times. One difficulty is that some members, especially ministers and junior

Treasury in Liverpool's government, believed that if the resources of government were further reduced it would be 'quite impossible for *any* set of men to conduct the government of this country'. 'No government', Wellington lamented in 1830, 'can go on without some means of rewarding services (to the King in parliament). I have absolutely none.' During the debates on the Reform Bill in March 1831, Sir Robert Harry Inglis, after maintaining that at no time in George IV's reign did the number of placemen in the House, including army and navy officers, exceed 109, censured 'the present ministers' because 'by a continual reduction of places in the gift of the Sovereign, they are diminishing the little influence which has been left to that Estate. . . . There might have been, at one time, some pretence for the charge that the House of Commons was filled with the creatures of the King; that time has long since passed.'

Many of these complaints recognize, if only by implication, that the decline of influence owed little to the passing of Place Acts. Indeed, the unenthusiastic reception accorded to Whitbread's motion of June 1809, calling for the exclusion of certain groups of placemen from the House of Commons, suggests that even reformers admitted that the King's influence in the House of Commons had decreased, and found the cry for exclusion of placemen out of date. This was partly, no doubt, because there were fewer placemen to exclude, and partly because, since reformers were not able to agree with ministers that the

ministers, held several places and are sometimes counted more than once; another is that the term 'placeman' is not precise — pensioners, contractors, army and navy officers, lords lieutenant, even legal officers, are not always counted as placemen. For example, Hawkesbury's figures exclude army and navy officers and perhaps legal officers. It is, on this basis, possible to compare his figure of 52, for 1800, with that of 51 for holders of English and Scottish offices in 1808 (cf. p. 106, footnote 1), and to compare both with Inglis's figure of 109, which includes about 20 Irish office-holders and about 30 army and navy officers. Some discrepancies must remain, since those who quote figures seldom explain them, but the general picture of serious decline, in the fifty years before the Reform Act, is indisputable.

King's influence as a whole was dangerously diminished, they tended to look elsewhere than the House of Commons for evidence of its exercise. They believed that such evidence could be found in the constituencies. Thus Curwen, for example, introduced into the Commons in 1809 a Bill, which became law, for 'the better securing of the Independence and Purity of Parliament, by preventing the procuring or obtaining of seats by corrupt practices'. Nevertheless, it seems clear that the lack of interest in the exclusion of placemen from the House of Commons was not simply because there were fewer of them. Whitbread's proposal would have excluded from the House, unconditionally, most junior ministers, certain Household officers, pensioners for life and sinecurists. It was opposed, by Whigs as well as Tories, not only on the practical grounds that the influence of the crown over the House of Commons was no longer large enough to justify a Place Bill, but also on theoretical grounds. 'Before the Revolution', said Ponsonby, 'the government was conducted out of parliament; but since the Revolution the practice of the constitution was, that it should be conducted in parliament, and principally in that House. It was essential, therefore, that the servants of the government should be there in person.' The *Edinburgh Review*, in July 1807, had gone further than this. While asserting that 'the influence of the Executive is . . . the great evil which infects our constitution', it had boldly declared that placemen 'are better in parliament than anywhere else' and that to exclude them 'would not have the effect of reducing influence'. It contended further that to exclude 'the official advisers of the Sovereign' was absurd, and that 'sinecure offices and pensions' were 'mere trifles . . . too inconsiderable to deserve any distinguished notice in the general estimate of patronage'.

The King's infringement of the Septennial convention in the period 1784–1832 tilted the balance between King and Commons in favour of the King, and so might have been expected in some measure to offset the disturbance of the balance in favour of the Commons, by the decline of influence. Any effect of this kind was only temporary. Infringement of the Septennial convention was certainly intended as an alleviation of the difficulties of managing the Commons, for such infringement enabled the King to choose the time for general elections, and, if he wished, to endow new ministers with a new House of Commons. In practice, however, the triumphant success of the general election of 1784, the first seriously premature general election, was not repeated by any of its successors. In spite of its great dangers in theory, therefore, infringement of the Septennial convention came in the end only to emphasize that the dearth of patronage made it difficult for the King to enable his ministers to win general elections as well as to manage the House of Commons.

Before the Reform Act, then, the relation between King and Commons was changing. The balance between them was imperilled by the greater independence of the Commons which resulted from the decline of influence, and the King's infringement of the Septennial convention proved an incomplete answer to this decline. That the balance was not entirely destroyed was due to the growth in cabinet solidarity and in the strength of the prime minister in the same period. This growth certainly strengthened the executive in relation to the Commons. On the other hand, it did not really strengthen the King in relation to the Commons, for it also had the effect of strengthening the King's ministers at the expense of the King, and this underlined his dependence on them rather than their dependence on him.

Most of the developments of the period 1784 to 1832 were pushed further by the Reform Act. For the effect of its abolition of rotten boroughs, its increase of county representation, and its creation of a more uniform fran-

chise, was to make general elections even more unpre-
dictable and the management of the House of Commons
by old methods even more difficult. The balance between
King and Commons, already endangered by the decline
of patronage, ceased to exist though it did not cease to
be extolled. Moreover, the unpredictability of general
elections made it improbable that the King could change
the House of Commons to the advantage of ministers he
liked, and this made it difficult for him to change his
ministers without reference to the existing House.

Yet the Reform Act did not simply set the seal on the
Commons' victory over the King, any more than the
process of administrative reform in the fifty years before
the Act had simply strengthened the Commons at the
expense of the King. For the weakening of the influence
of the King and individual peers over the constituencies
was also a step towards making the Commons, as well as
the King, or rather the King's ministers, dependent on the
electorate, a power not included in the eighteenth-century
constitutional balance at all.

This process in the end forced the King out of politics,
for it deprived him of the free choice of his prime minister
as well as of his other ministers. At the same time, it
linked the Commons and the King's ministers together in
a new way, and more tightly than ever before, because it
necessitated the choosing of the King's ministers immediately after and in conformity with the results of a general
election. This was a time-connection of a new kind. But
the end of this process was not reached even in practice,
far less in theory, before 1867. In 1832, and for more than
a generation afterwards, the choice of ministers by the
King, and the choice of the House of Commons by the
electorate, remained in theory separate events. If a change
of ministers sometimes followed closely on a general
election, it never followed directly, and a connection
between the two events was not admitted in theory.

Ministers still did not resign in response to a defeat at a general election, but they tended to resign, more often than they had done before 1832, in response to a defeat in the House of Commons. This was partly because, after 1832, a defeat in the House was sometimes the aftermath of defeat at a general election, whereas before 1832 a defeat in the House was usually due to the adverse opinion of the House on a particular measure. Moreover, the possibility of electoral defeat, and the knowledge that ministers could not count on improving their position by means of a premature general election, made it less easy for ministers to disregard defeats in the House.

CHAPTER V

THE HOUSE OF COMMONS
AND THE KING'S SERVANTS

BETWEEN 1660 and 1832 the King's choice of servants and the electorate's choice of the House of Commons were two distinct processes. The relationship between the Commons and the King's servants was therefore primarily an extension of the relationship between the Commons and the King : the Commons could not hope to influence or control the King's measures unless they could in some degree influence or control his choice of men. They did not in the period 1660 to 1832 succeed in doing this, except in so far as the King found it expedient that his ministers should on the whole be acceptable to the House of Commons. This indirect limitation on his choice, which was present throughout the whole period, was, for most of it, partly offset by the existence of patronage sufficient to assist the ministers of the King's choice both in managing the Commons and in ensuring that general elections strengthened their own position in the House. The decline of patronage after 1784 weakened and finally destroyed this advantage, but it did not destroy the theory that ministers were the King's, nor did it turn them into designates of the Commons. In theory, indeed, the House of Commons was still chosen to suit ministers previously chosen by the King not only in the years of declining influence from 1784 to 1832 but for at least a generation after 1832. The only change in the early nineteenth century was that ministers began to be expected to resign after a defeat in the House of Commons, not merely because they had lost the favour of the Commons, but also in order to save the King from the possibility of defeat at a general election for ministers who enjoyed his confidence. Yet ministers did not always resign after a defeat in the Commons, even after 1832. Electoral defeat for the King's ministers was a possibility only after the decline of patronage; before its decline, defeats in the House of Commons were not normally followed by resignation, still less by dissolution.

During the whole of the period 1660–1832 the real limitation of the King's choice of ministers came less from the Commons than from the ministers themselves. Accordingly, the greatest change in this period was not in the relationship between the Commons and the King's servants but in the relationship between the King and his servants. Even here, the change was indirect : it lay in essence in the emergence of a more defined and mainly ministerial cabinet, with an acknowledged chief minister. This chief minister imposed some degree of unity on the cabinet as a result of his increasing share in choosing it, but he remained himself the King's choice. To some extent, indeed, his position as the King's minister was emphasized by the fact that the King chose him in order that he might, subject to the King's wishes, form a government. This changed relationship between the King and his servants was an essential factor in the later transformation of the relationship between the Commons and the King's servants. Ultimately, the King's servants became the servants of the Commons and, at the same time, the agents of the majority in the Commons, chosen immediately after and in accordance with the result of a general election. This transformation, however, took place not before but after 1832.

The relationship of the Commons with the King's servants was an acute problem before the Civil War. To the Long Parliament it seemed that the fundamental reason for friction between King and parliament was the King's employment of advisers and ministers whose deliberate policy was 'to foment jealousies between the King and Parliament'. The Commons were aware that impeachment, even if it forced the King to dismiss his advisers, could not fully solve this problem. Accordingly, in December 1641, the Grand Remonstrance did not merely demand that the King should choose such advisers and ministers 'as the Parliament may have cause to confide in', but insisted, in addition, that 'the Commons may have just cause to take exceptions at some men for being councillors' although they were not willing or able to impeach these men for legal crimes. The Nineteen Propositions sent to the King at York in June 1642 demanded, more explicitly, that ministers of state and privy councillors should be chosen by approbation of parliament, and that privy councillors should be required to take an oath prescribed by Act of Parliament. The Commons did not make good their claim to control the King's choice of ministers and advisers. It is true that, in November 1647, Charles I went so far as to intimate to the Speaker of the House of Lords that he was willing to consent to an Act of Parliament providing that, for the rest of his reign, all officers of state and privy councillors should be named by parliament. Nothing came of this, however, and the Commons' claim was not renewed at the Restoration. The Commons were therefore, after 1660, in the same position as they had been in 1640: their control over the King's servants was limited to the power of impeaching them or threatening to do so. Impeachment became a less precarious weapon when, after 1689, the need for annual meetings of parliament made it more difficult for the King to frustrate impeachments by dissolving parliament, and when, after 1701, they could not be stopped by a royal pardon. Nevertheless, impeachment remained a judicial and extraordinary act, not a method of regulating the normal relation between the Commons and the King's servants. Such an act was not really adaptable — even when it took the form of a threat — either to the Commons' aim of persuading the King to choose servants acceptable to the Commons, or to their aim of persuading the King's servants to pursue a policy approved by the Commons.

Indeed, it was not easy to prescribe a normal relationship between the Commons and the King's servants either by legislation or by injunction. An attempt to do so was made in 1701. But both the clauses of the Act of Settlement which affected the relations between the Commons and the King's servants — the Place Clause and the Privy Council Clause — were withdrawn before 1714, and impeachment remained, under the Hanoverians, the only legal way in which the Commons could hope to control the King's servants.

The Place Clause, which excluded all crown officeholders from the House of Commons, was repealed in 1705 and superseded by clauses in the Succession to the Crown Acts of 1705 and 1707 which included ministers among the placemen who, provided they obtained re-election, were allowed to sit in the House. Nevertheless, few eighteenth-century governments had more than two or three ministers in the House of Commons, and, from this point of view, the modification of the 1701 Place Clause was of vital importance only to the minister responsible for finance, the First Lord of the Treasury, who either sat in the Commons himself or, if he was a peer, had the Chancellor of the Exchequer there to deputize for him. It is, of course, true that joint ministerial responsibility to the Commons was ultimately linked with the presence of ministers in the House, but this later development can hardly be attributed to the Place Clauses in the Acts of 1705 and 1707, which were concerned primarily not with ministers but with influence.

On the other hand, the Privy Council Clause in the

Act of Settlement was concerned directly with the problem of increasing the Commons' control over the King's advisers. It proposed to do so by reviving the Privy Council, depriving the King of all sources of advice except the Privy Council and ensuring that the Commons should know what advice it gave. The clause required that all matters 'relating to the well governing of this Kingdom which are properly cognizable in the Privy Council by the Laws and Customs of the Realm shall be transacted there and all Resolutions taken there shall be signed by such of the Privy Council as shall advise and consent to the same'. The clause was repealed in 1705, not because the House of Commons had repented of its desire to control the King's servants but because it was clearly impracticable to do so in this way, 'since it was visible, that no man would be a privy-counsellor on those terms'.

Indeed, the Commons' hope of controlling the King's servants by controlling the Privy Council, and forcing the King to take advice from it, had been impracticable even in Charles II's reign. In theory the Privy Council was restored in 1660 to its old position, except with regard to its judicial powers, so that it seemed again to be, as it was described in every edition of the *Present State of England* and of the *Present State of Great Britain*, from 1669 to 1755, 'the *Primum Mobile* of the Civil Government of *England*, from whence all the inferior *Orbs* derive their Motion'. It is clear, however, that this was an illusion, and that in fact the Privy Council never, after 1660, recovered its former position either as advisory or as executive instrument of government. The most obvious sign of its waning power was its increasing size. The number of Privy Councillors was 30 in 1660 and 50 in 1675; it was reduced to 33 in 1679, as a result of Charles's reform of the Privy Council, but by 1685 it had risen to 45. The increase continued throughout the eighteenth century: there were 51 privy councillors in 1700, 82 in 1712, 106 in 1782, 131

— more than four times as many as in 1660 — in 1801.

In the 1670s the House of Commons began to complain that the King was taking advice on important matters of state neither from parliament nor from the Privy Council but from a cabinet or cabinet council, a small and secret group of confidential advisers. In 1678 the 'Cabinet Council, that takes things out of the hands of the Privy Council' was thought to be responsible for Charles's rejection of a militia Bill, and in 1679 Charles tried to disarm further criticism by remodelling the Privy Council and promising that, in future, he would govern with its constant advice, and would 'lay aside the use he may have hitherto made of any single ministry or private advices or Foreign Committees for the general direction of his affairs'. Charles did not keep his promise, and James II and William III continued the practice of taking advice from groups other than the Privy Council. In 1691 it was stated in the House of Commons that in the past 'Kings consulted with their Privy-Councils; formerly they went not into cabals', and in 1694 it was suggested that William's refusal of the royal assent to the Place Bill was due to the advice of his Cabinet Council. The critics took their stand on the constitution: cabinet councils were said to be 'a Device of foreign extraction and unknown to the Laws of the Land', designed to upset the constitution by increasing the King's power at the expense of the people. In 1701 Sir Humphrey Mackworth, in the *Vindication of the Rights of the Commons of England*, declared that it was an 'Innovation of Evil Ministers, that War and Peace, and Matters of the highest Consequences, should be finally Conducted in a Secret Cabal, and only pass through the Privy-Council for Forms Sake, as a Conduit-Pipe, to convey those Resolutions with authority to the People. . . . 'Tis therefore a Noble Resolution in His Majesty to Restore to *England* the Practice of the Ancient Constitution . . . and not only to

Declare, but Debate and Transact all Matters of State in the Privy Council.'

In spite of the Commons' claims to be conservative, there was in reality little justification for their contention that the King had no constitutional right to consult any man or group of men except the Privy Council, and the Commons were certainly taking to themselves a new power when, in the clause of the Act of Settlement praised by Mackworth, they tried to force the King not only to consult the Privy Council but also to make known to the Commons the names of those councillors who had recommended particular policies. The making of this claim no doubt hastened rather than delayed the decline of the Privy Council, for no King would take advice and no men would give him advice on these conditions. Before the end of the seventeenth century the Privy Council had ceased to be an advisory body. Its functions had become ceremonial and formal: instead of taking decisions itself it registered decisions taken by other bodies, by the cabinet, by a government department, or by one of its own committees.

The cabinet, or cabinet council, was a group of confidential servants who advised the King on important matters of general policy and was therefore the heir of the advisory functions of the Privy Council. The existence of such a body, and the King's right to consult it, was not after 1705 seriously threatened by the Commons, but the cabinet was, nevertheless, not accepted as a part of the constitution in the same way as the Privy Council was. The Cabinet is not mentioned in any of the editions of Chamberlayne's *Present State of Great-Britain*.[1] In 1726, however, the author of the *True State of England* remarked, in the section dealing with the Privy Council, which he described as 'generally composed of the most eminent

---

[1] Nor is it mentioned by Blackstone. In a book devoted to an examination of the laws, however, the significance of this neglect (as of the neglect to discuss the parliamentary function of patronage) is perhaps not great.

Persons in the Kingdom, fit to advise His Majesty upon all Emergencies', that 'The King may declare to, or conceal from his *Privy Counsellors* whatever he thinks fit; and has a select *Council* out of their Number, commonly called, *The Cabinet Council*, with whom his Majesty determines such Affairs as are most Important, and require the utmost Secrecy'. As late as February 1770 Thomas Townshend, in the House of Commons, referred to the cabinet as a 'midnight assembly', while William Beckford described it as 'an unlawful assembly', and, in defending the cabinet from these charges, Richard Rigby went only so far as to claim that 'the cabinet is well-known to consist of a committee or a few members of the privy council called together for particular purposes; it is not pretended to have any constitutional authority, but it does not therefore follow, that it may not deliberate on measures to be referred to the privy council that has'.[1] Even in 1806 Castlereagh found it necessary to protest in the House of Commons that the cabinet was 'as well known to Parliament as if the existence of such a Council had been an object of express legislative provision'. That it remained possible, for so much of the eighteenth century, to maintain that the cabinet was a body 'unknown to the constitution' was because the cabinet was in fact unknown to the law, because its composition was indefinite, because the members of the cabinet did not enter and leave it at the same time, and because their connection with each other remained undefined and fluctuating.

In the long run there is no doubt that the consolidation of the cabinet — especially the development towards political uniformity of its members, towards the idea that all its members should hold office for the same period, and

---

[1] Rigby's definition is, to say the least, a cautious one. It is quite clear that by 1770 the cabinet discussed many subjects which were not afterwards referred to the Privy Council. But, of course, cabinet decisions involving certain kinds of executive action went to the Privy Council for the issue of an order in council.

towards the abandonment of the idea that all ministers were equal and communicated direct with the King — restricted the King's freedom in choosing his ministers. In the short run, however, these developments were not always discouraged by the King, and not always opposed by the Commons, since, though they certainly tended to strengthen the executive, they did not always seem to weaken the Commons. The consolidation of the cabinet was a slow process not, primarily, because either King or Commons consistently opposed it, but because the members of the cabinet did so. The basis for consolidation, which was achieved by the end of the eighteenth century, was the normal identification of the members of the cabinet with the most important ministers of state and the shedding of non-official members. The development towards this identification was not opposed by the Commons.

As soon as the composition of the cabinet became at all clearly defined, in William III's reign, there seems to have been a connection between membership of the cabinet and office-holding. Sunderland, in 1701, maintained that the holders of certain offices had 'in some sort a right to enter (the cabinet council) by their employment' — the Archbishop of Canterbury, the Lord Chancellor, the Lord High Steward, the Lord Chamberlain, the First Lord of the Treasury, the two Secretaries of State, and, if the King wished, the First Lord of the Admiralty and the Master General of the Ordnance. These men did in fact sit in the cabinet councils of Anne's reign, but they soon came to include also other Household officials — frequently the Groom of the Stole and the Master of the Horse — the Lord Privy Seal, the Lord Chief Justice, and the Lord Lieutenant of Ireland, and perhaps one or two peers or politicians who did not hold important office but were personally important. The total of fourteen or fifteen at the beginning of George I's reign increased to sixteen or seventeen in George II's reign and twenty-one

at the beginning of George III's reign. They were summoned by the King and presided over either by him, or,
in his absence, by the Lord President of the Council.
Groups of this kind, representing Church, State, and
Household, were imposing assemblies but too large and
mixed to be business-like, and it seems that even before
the end of Anne's reign the more important ministers met
together informally, apart from the larger body and apart
from the Queen, discussing business and coming to decisions which were later taken to and endorsed by the whole
cabinet council. This inner ring of five, six, or seven
ministers contained always the First Lord of the Treasury
and the two Secretaries of State, usually the Lord President
of the Council and the Lord Chancellor, and often one or
two others who varied according to the business in hand,
for example the First Lord of the Admiralty. By the late
1730s it met regularly once a week, and came to be called
the 'efficient', 'effective', or 'confidential' cabinet. The
whole cabinet council, now called the 'nominal' cabinet,
had, by the middle of the eighteenth century, grown so
large and ineffective that the rank of cabinet councillor,
Horace Walpole said in 1761, would soon be 'indistinct
from Privy Counsellor by growing as numerous'.

In George II's reign decisions of policy taken by the
small ministerial group still had to be endorsed by the
whole cabinet. By the early part of George III's reign
this was no longer so. The nominal members of the
cabinet did not receive important state papers, and they
retained only two regular functions: they met before the
opening and proroguing of parliament to hear the King's
Speech read, and they met to advise the King on death
sentences. After the 1770s there are few references to
nominal cabinet councillors and, in practice, the identification of 'cabinet' with 'most important ministers' seems to
have been almost complete before Pitt's first administration.
When, in 1801, Addington declared that the cabinet should

contain only the most important ministers he was describing the normal practice and not only the ideal at the end of the eighteenth century. Walpole's cabinet seldom contained fewer than 16 members, and there were 21 in 1761. There seems to have been some attempt at reduction in the 1760s : Chatham's cabinet of 1767 contained only 14 and North's apparently had only 9. Rockingham's and Shelburne's cabinets both contained 11 members. The Fox–North cabinet of April 1783 seems to have contained only 7 members, and Pitt's cabinet of December 1783 began with 6 : the First Lord of the Treasury (who was also Chancellor of the Exchequer), the First Lord of the Admiralty, two Secretaries of State, the Lord President of the Council, and the Lord Chancellor. The reduction did not last : membership of the cabinet did not exceed 9 before 1793, but it rose to 13 in 1794, by the inclusion of the Secretary for War, the Secretary at War, the Commander-in-Chief of the Army, and one minister without portfolio. For the rest of Pitt's administration the number of members of the cabinet did not again fall below 10. Addington's cabinet in 1801 contained only 9 members, but after a few months increased to 11, Pitt's in 1804 contained 12, and, until 1832, 13 was the average number. The smallest cabinet between 1804 and 1832 was Wellington's of 1828, which had 11 members, and several cabinets had a membership as large as 15.

The evolution of a working cabinet, composed normally of the most important ministers, with occasionally the addition of a minister without portfolio, did not have a large immediate effect on the relation between the Commons and the King's servants. The development was not opposed by the King, for it seemed to strengthen the cabinet without in any way restricting the King's freedom to choose its members. Nor was this development in itself consistently opposed by the Commons, for it had the advantage of making the composition of the cabinet less fluid. To the Commons the safeguards against strong cabinets lay rather in the fact that cabinets were not united in opinion, in the fact that their members were not appointed and dismissed at the same time, and, above all, in the fact that they had no recognized leader, and the Commons' opposition was therefore directed against developments which seemed to threaten these safeguards, and especially the last one. The Commons' dislike of an 'overgrown' minister, who was, it was thought, necessarily a 'court minister', was made more effective because it was shared by the cabinet itself, whose members were jealous of any minister who seemed to monopolize the King's confidence. In theory all ministers were equally the King's servants and individually accountable for their actions to the King and to Parliament; and the theory was reinforced by the fact that cabinets were not politically homogeneous and that their members were not appointed and dismissed at the same time. A change of administration normally meant that three or four ministers were replaced and others changed their offices. For example, on Walpole's resignation in 1742 only three ministers were replaced, and on Newcastle's resignation in 1762 only two ministers were replaced. George I's reign inevitably began with a complete change of administration, and an almost complete change was forced on George III in March 1782 and again in April 1783, but these were exceptions. George III considered that 'naming the ministers to be employed' was one of the two prerogatives left to the crown — the other, which he never used, was refusing the royal assent to Bills passed by both Houses — and, like his predecessors, he thought that the way to preserve this prerogative was to choose 'mixed', non-party ministries, and so avoid the possibility of being dictated to. Of all his predecessors William III had been most successful in this aim, and George III took William as his model in this as in other things.

The King was, in fact, more anxious to insist on 'mixed' cabinets, which seemed to guarantee his independence, than he was to prevent one member of the cabinet from assuming preponderance over his colleagues. Indeed, it was to some extent convenient for the King that one minister, and the same one, should preside over cabinet meetings and convey to the King the result of his ministers' deliberations, and it is clear that the King did not, at any time in the period 1660–1832, consider that he was thereby precluded from asking other ministers individually and separately for their advice. Opposition to a preponderant minister came in the first place from the other ministers, and in the second place from the Commons. This opposition, though persistent, had in the end to yield to the fact that there was, in every cabinet, one minister who, by virtue of his office, held a stronger position than his colleagues both in relation to the King and in relation to the House of Commons. This was the First Lord of the Treasury. As early as 1726 the author of the *True State of England* wrote that the 'Lord High Treasurer is generally said to be the King's Prime Minister Judicatory between the Sovereign and his people'.[1] General recognition came later. By 1783, however, it was generally admitted both that one member of the cabinet enjoyed precedence over his colleagues and commanded the especial confidence of the King, and that this was usually the First Lord of the Treasury. Walpole was certainly

---

[1] The Treasury had been in commission since the beginning of George I's reign. But since the author of the *True State of England* was one of the first to regard the cabinet as part of the constitution it seems probable that he did not regard Walpole's position as fundamentally different from that of a Lord High Treasurer. Indeed, the violent attacks both on the cabinet and on the prime minister in the 1730s and 1740s were primarily Bolingbroke's, and later Pitt's, platform of attack on Walpole. The organ of attack in the 1730s was the *Craftsman*. In 1741 *The Champion* condemned the office of prime minister as 'pernicious and incompatible with that Balance of Power' necessary to 'the National Liberties' and in 1742 the *Westminster Journal* declared that 'of all the odious characters that ever debased the human species, none . . . has been so universally detested as that of a wicked, overgrown Prime Minister'.

the strongest of the ministers who formed the cabinet in the 1730s: he denied that he was a prime minister partly because prime minister meant 'court minister', partly because in theory all ministers were equal. By contrast, Lord North's denial that he was a prime minister was made with regret, and accompanied by a clear statement of the desirability that there should be a prime minister. In 1778 North begged the King to allow him to resign because 'in critical times, it is necessary that there should be one directing Minister, who should plan the whole of the operations of government, and controul all the other departments of administration, so far as to make them co-operate zealously and actively with his designs even tho' contrary to their own' and 'he is certainly not capable of being such a minister as he has described'. Again, in 1783, when discussing with Fox the coalition's attitude to the King, North said 'If you mean . . . that there should not be a Government of Departments, I agree with you. I think it a very bad thing. . . . However, the Government of Departments was not brought about by me when I came into His Majesty's Government. I found it so, and I am ready to confess that I had not sufficient vigour and resolution to put an end to it.' Nevertheless, North insisted that his government had not been unduly dependent on the King: 'though the Government in my time was a Government of Departments, yet the whole was done by Ministers except in a few instances'.

Pitt's opinion that 'there should be an avowed and real Minister, possessing the chief weight in the Council, and the principal place in the confidence of the King' makes no advance on North's except for the assertion that 'that Minister ought . . . to be the person at the head of the finances'. Pitt's opinion is, however, interesting because it was expressed in 1803 to Melville, in response to a suggestion by Addington that the cabinet should be reconstructed, with real power in the hands of Pitt and Addington, as Secretaries of State, and only nominal power in the hands of Lord Chatham, as First Lord of the Treasury. An arrangement of this kind would have followed exactly the pattern of the coalition of 1783, when Fox and North had the power and Portland had the position, and it is not surprising that Pitt refused. Nevertheless, although Pitt's statement was made in reply to a proposal that he should participate in a particular kind of government, it undoubtedly represents his general opinion. He, like North, was concerned principally with the relation of a prime minister to the other ministers, and not with his relation either to the King — whose confidence was the essential basis of his prime minister's position — or to the Commons. Pitt was certain that there could be 'no rivalry or division of power' in the cabinet, and that 'if it should unfortunately come to such a radical difference of opinion that no spirit of conciliation or concession can reconcile, the sentiments of the Minister must be allowed and understood to prevail, leaving the other ministers to act as they may conceive themselves conscientiously called upon to act under such circumstances'. Here — in the prime minister's relations with other ministers — North's theory was, on the whole, Pitt's practice. None the less, it seems that differences within Pitt's cabinets were often met in fact not by Pitt's overriding his colleagues but by his deciding that he was not strong enough to press them. This was undoubtedly true of certain cabinet differences on the conduct of the war, and it is most unlikely that Pitt could have forced his colleagues, let alone the Commons, to accept Catholic emancipation unless, perhaps, the King had been decidedly in favour of it. Pitt's theory, then, has nothing new except his opinion that the First Lord of the Treasury should be the first Minister. Indeed, once the position of first minister was accepted, it could hardly be disputed, at least in theory, that the First Lord of the Treasury was its most suitable occupant. Finance above all tied the King and his ministers to the Commons, and the First Lord had, either in his own person or through his deputy, a commanding position in the Commons. This position was rendered unassailable by the fact that his supervision of the patronage at the disposal of the Treasury made the management of the Commons and of elections peculiarly his concern. The decline of patronage after 1784, which made the management of the Commons and of elections more difficult, made it, for that reason, even more important.

Although the recognition that one member of the cabinet was in a superior position was not in itself necessarily inconvenient for the King, the recognition was bound to affect his choice of the other members of the cabinet, and in the end it deprived him of this choice. Indeed, long before there was general acceptance of the idea that every administration must have a prime minister, a strong minister inevitably exercised some influence over the choice of some of his colleagues. This influence was sometimes resented by the King, but not always, since it certainly tended to make administration smoother. Walpole, for example, demanded and obtained the inclusion in the cabinet of some of his political adherents, and so did Newcastle, Chatham, and North. Rockingham's ability, in 1782, to force George III to replace nearly all the members of North's administration was, of course, resented. In the event, however, this dictation of a cabinet by its chief member, in defiance of the King's wishes, was so radical that it weakened instead of strengthening Rockingham's position. The Fox–North ministry was weak for the same reason. The younger Pitt's influence on the choice of his colleagues was wide, not because he himself was strong but because George III wished above all to get rid of the supporters of Fox, North, and Portland. Even so it was not until 1792 that Pitt was able to prevail upon the King to dismiss Thurlow, who had been the

'King's man' in the cabinet and never trusted by Pitt, by threatening to resign himself if Thurlow stayed. It is true enough that during the rest of his reign George III usually accepted his prime ministers' choice of colleagues, and that George IV and William IV seldom refused to do so. Their occasional intervention was, however, generally regarded as perfectly constitutional, though it might be inconvenient, and it remained effective. Fox only emerged from his long opposition in 1806 because there was no alternative to a Grenville government; Grey remained excluded from office for the whole of George IV's reign; George IV in 1821 refused Liverpool's request that Canning should enter the cabinet, and, in 1827, against the wishes of Goderich, appointed Herries as Chancellor of the Exchequer. The King's normal acceptance of ministers recommended by his prime minister had as its corollary a tendency for a larger number of cabinet ministers to be appointed at the same time. Again, however, there was no rapid or uninterrupted development in the period 1784–1832 from partial to complete changes of administration: in 1806 the *Annual Register* regarded 'a thorough and complete change in all the departments of the state' as unusual, and it remained unusual later in the period. Although there were ten new ministers at the beginning of Pitt's ministry in 1783, and eleven at the beginning of Grenville's in 1806, Portland's in 1807, and Grey's in 1830, there were only five, on average, at the beginning of the other seven ministries between 1783 and 1830. Even five, however, was larger than the normal average turnover before 1783.[1]

Both these developments strengthened the prime minister in relation to his colleagues. He remained, notwithstanding, the King's minister, and in theory the King's

[1] Approximate figures from 1742 to 1783 are: 1742, three; 1744, five; 1746, two; 1754, three; 1756, five; 1757, three; 1762, two; 1763, three; 1765, eight; July 1766, eight; August 1766, six; 1767, four; 1770, two; March 1782, ten; July 1782, three; April 1783, nine.

choice was not more restricted in the period 1784–1832 than it was in the period 1716–83. Pitt's criticism of the Commons' attempts to force the King to remove him in 1784 did not differ from Walpole's criticism in 1741, though the circumstances differed in that Pitt was newly appointed, in the teeth of the House of Commons, while Walpole had been in office twenty years. Both criticisms were orthodox doctrine. Indeed, no one but an opposition, bent on opposing, ever denied that such attempts were an unwarrantable and unconstitutional infringement of the King's prerogative, and that his right to choose his ministers without reference to the House of Commons implied a right to keep them for as long as seemed good to him, if necessary against the wishes of the Commons. Sandys, in February 1741, putting the motion for an address from the Commons to the King, asking him to dismiss Walpole, asserted that 'no sovereign of these Kingdoms ought to employ any minister who is disagreeable to the people, and when any minister is become unpopular, it is our duty to inform the King, that he may give general satisfaction by his removal'; Fox, in March 1784, proposed that the House send an address to the King, informing him 'that the continuance of an administration, which does not possess the confidence of the representative of the people, must be injurious to the public service'. Walpole's reply, claiming that 'an address to his majesty to remove one of his servants, without so much as alledging any particular crime against him, is one of the greatest encroachments that was ever made upon the prerogatives of the crown', was unexceptionable. Pitt's reply only elaborates Walpole's. Pitt admitted that 'such a sentiment of disapprobation (by the House of Commons) surely placed ministers in awkward and unpleasant situations; but that it should force them to retire he maintained was an unconstitutional doctrine, hostile to the prerogative of the crown, and to that balance of power, on which the excellency of our government depended. . . . It is the intention of this address to arrogate a power which does not belong to the House of Commons — to place a negative on the exercise of the prerogative, and to destroy the balance of power in the government as it was settled at the revolution.' The 1741 motion was defeated by 290 votes to 106; the 1784 motion was carried by 201 votes to 189, and three weeks later parliament was dissolved.

Other attempts by the Commons before 1832 to influence or to censure the King's choice of ministers were not numerous. On 15 April 1807, after the dismissal of Grenville, W. H. Lyttelton moved in the House of Commons a resolution 'that the House, considering a firm and efficient administration as indispensably necessary, in the present important crisis of public affairs, has seen with the deepest regret, the late change in his majesty's councils'. The resolution was defeated by 244 votes to 198, and there followed within a fortnight a prorogation of parliament and an announcement that the King intended as soon as possible to recur to the sense of his people. On 21 May 1812, after the death of Perceval, the Commons carried a motion, proposed by Stuart Wortley and seconded by Lord Milton, for an address to the Prince Regent asking him 'to form a strong and efficient Administration'. The Commons' address was widely regarded as an unconstitutional interference with the prerogative of the crown. Wilberforce, for example, opposed it in the Commons on this ground, maintaining that 'the question whether the House should have a previous negative on the appointment of ministers' had been raised and decided in 1784, and that although the present motion did not explicitly 'prescribe to the prince whom he should choose', it did so by implication. The Regent did, as a result of the address, investigate the possibility of a government based on the union of parties, but his negotiations were not successful. At the beginning of June Liverpool was confirmed in office and the Commons negatived, without a division, a motion by Stuart Wortley for an address to the Regent regretting that he had not yet complied with the wishes of the House. It was natural that greater success should attend an address from the Commons to the King during the Reform Bill crisis of May 1832. On 10 May, after Grey had resigned as a result of his defeat in the House of Lords, the Commons carried, by 288 votes to 208, Lord Ebrington's motion for an address to the King begging him 'to call to his councils such persons only as will carry into effect, unimpaired, that bill for the reform of the representation of the people which has recently passed this House'. Yet even here, though the King recalled Grey and promised to create enough peers to carry the Bill in the Lords, his negotiations with Wellington and Peel show clearly enough that the Commons' wishes were not the prime reason for the King's surrender.

In general practice, too, it is not clear that the King's choice of first minister was more restricted in the period 1784–1832 than in the earlier period. The choice of Pitt in 1783, without regard to the opinions of the Commons, was paralleled by the dismissal of Grenville and the recall of Pitt's friends to office, under Portland, in 1807. It was also paralleled, though to a lesser extent, by the retention of Liverpool, appointed as First Lord of the Treasury after Perceval's death at the beginning of May 1812, in spite of the Commons' attempt to force the Regent to appoint an all-party government (including supporters of Catholic emancipation) and get rid of the remnants of Pitt's friends. It was not doubted that George IV would have been perfectly within his constitutional rights if he had dismissed Liverpool in 1820, or at any time during the 1820s, as he almost certainly would have done if he had been able to find a substitute both congenial and willing to serve. Canning and Goderich were George IV's choice in 1827, though he was unwilling to take the responsibility of choosing Canning, and Wellington was his choice in 1828. Moreover, William IV's dismissal of Melbourne and appointment of Peel in 1834 was not generally regarded as unconstitutional. There was, however, one important change in practice in the period which began in 1784 : the King's choice was sometimes related in time to a general election, and this proved in the end to be dangerous because it coincided with a shrinkage in the patronage which ensured that general elections should be beneficial to the ministers under whose auspices they were held. Before this danger became obvious, the closer relationship in time between choice of ministers and choice of House of Commons seemed rather to increase the King's freedom of choice of ministers, for it reduced the effectiveness of any opinion the Commons might have about the King's ministers. The new relationship was a natural corollary of the highly successful premature general election of March 1784, which followed the King's dismissal of ministers congenial to the Commons and the appointment in their place of ministers congenial to the King but disliked by the Commons.[1] The dissolution was a spectacular assertion of the King's right to choose his ministers without reference to the Commons, and his right was confirmed in practice when the election gave his chosen ministers a favourable House of Commons.

Many conclusions have been drawn from the general election of 1784. The inescapable conclusion, and the one which most impressed contemporaries, is that the King could, both in theory and in practice, choose his own

[1] The combination of a change of ministers and a dissolution was considered before Pitt's appointment and not as a result of it. In the summer of 1783 Temple advised the King not to dismiss his ministers immediately but to wait, since they were likely to get less rather than more popular. He prophesied that the King 'might look forward to a change of his ministers in the autumn ; and that, as the last resource, a dissolution of this Parliament, chosen by Lord North and occasionally filled by Mr. Fox, might offer him the means of getting rid of the chains which pressed upon him' (Buckingham, *Courts and Cabinets of George III*, i. 304). The King suggested a dissolution to Pitt in January 1784 : it was Pitt who decided to wait.

ministers, and that ministers unpopular or defeated in the House of Commons need not resign provided they had the King's support, for the King's support would give them the electorate's support at the next general election and, thereafter, the support of a new House of Commons. The fact that, after choosing his ministers, George III anticipated the date of the next election, was perhaps an indirect sign of the growing desirability that the Commons should support ministers the King had chosen; but it is clear that the sign was only given in the knowledge that the Commons' support could be obtained by means of a general election. George III and Pitt did not need to wait for the normal date of the next general election because there was no doubt of the result. None the less, the fact that they did not wait, quite apart from the reason why they did not need to do so, put a new emphasis on the prerogative of dissolution, which had been little emphasized in the period of regular elections between 1716 and 1783, and especially on the value of dissolution as a postscript to a change of administration. General elections had, in the earlier period, been a defensive weapon in the hands of the King: they had never failed to improve the position of the King's existing ministers, but they had been held not in order to do so but at fairly regular intervals. Dissolution was, in the period 1784–1832, revealed as a powerful aggressive weapon in the hands of the King, for it was then shown to be a way of saving ministers from the consequences of defeats in the House of Commons, providing new ministers with a favourable House, and so changing ministers without regard to the wishes of the House. Dissolution as a deliberate postscript to a change of ministers seemed, in fact, to deny to the Commons not only all say in the King's choice of ministers but also all chance of effectively criticizing their policy when chosen. This denial was, ironically, made at the beginning of and during the period of declining influence; even so, it was not seriously challenged until the end of the period. The decline of influence gave the Commons more chance, in practice, of effectively criticizing the King's ministers, and in the last resort forcing their resignation, but it did not give them, in theory, any say in the choice of ministers.

The King's choice of first minister after 1784 was subject to a practical consideration : it was desirable that his minister should be acceptable to the House of Commons and able, either himself or by deputy, to provide it with competent leadership. This practical consideration was, of course, present before 1784, and, indeed, before 1716. But before 1784 it was to some extent offset by the King's influence on the creation of the House of Commons. In the period 1716–83 a general election was, in practice as well as in theory, not an appeal to the electorate to decide between two parties, or two policies, but an appeal to the electorate to give the King a House of Commons which would work with the King's ministers, or at least give them a fair trial. This appeal was made at more or less regular intervals, and it never resulted in the election of a House of Commons clearly less favourable to the existing government than the dissolved one had been.[1] After 1832 this position could not be maintained in practice : in 1835 the King's ministers did not gain enough seats to give them a majority, at a premature election held specifically in order to strengthen them ; in 1837 they obtained only a small majority, notwithstanding the support of a new monarch ; in 1841 they were badly defeated. In the intervening period, from 1784 to 1832, the earlier position was precariously held : the King's ministers did on occasion fail to derive any considerable benefit from a general election, but they were not actually defeated until 1830. This election could, with some justice, be regarded as abnormal, for, although parliamentary reform was not explicitly put before the electorate

[1] See p. 94 n.

as an issue for their decision — as it was in 1831 — the electorate was in fact much concerned with the question of reform, and both Wellington and Grey afterwards referred to the outcome of the election as the expression of the country's desire for reform. This expression, and even the controversy over the intrusion of an 'issue' as a factor in a general election, to some extent obscured the constitutional significance of an unprecedented defeat for the King's ministers. In this period, then, just as, within parliament, the decline of influence accentuated the value of strong personal leadership, so, outside parliament, the decline of influence accentuated the value of other methods of winning general elections. In this sphere, theory was called in to supplement failing practice.

It was, for this reason, primarily in the period 1784–1832 that the theory that a general election was an appeal from the King to the people 'to strengthen the hands of his ministers', and perhaps even to free him from a carping House of Commons, was emphasized and elaborated. It is clear that in fact the premature general elections of this period were personal appeals from the King to the electorate, over the head of the Commons. Equally, there can be no doubt that the increasing use of the King's name, in premature and in other elections, was beneficial to the King's ministers, and went some way towards counteracting the effect of the decline of patronage on the practice of electioneering. Ultimately, the inadequacy of the machinery which supported the theory of general elections certainly helped to produce a modification of the theory; the first result of the weakening of the machinery was, however, to make the theory more strongly insisted on. Accordingly, not only the period of the decline of influence, but also the aftermath of the Reform Act, which made the old practice of electioneering even more difficult, saw a tightening rather than a loosening of the old theory of electioneering. Contemporary comments on the general, elections of 1835, 1837, and 1841 make it abundantly clear that, although after 1832 governments no longer had the resources to win general elections, the idea that ministers congenial to the King ought not to be defeated at a general election was far from having been discarded. At all three elections, the electorate was explicitly asked to return a House of Commons favourable to ministers approved by the monarch. At the general election of 1841 Melbourne's Whig government was decisively defeated, not only in spite of the use of what remained of crown patronage, but also in spite of the Queen's passionate and expressed wish to retain the government. Even this did not kill the old idea that the purpose of a general election was not to choose a government. The conclusion generally drawn from the defeat of 1841 was that the prerogative of dissolution should be used with great care and not employed unless it was certain, on any particular occasion, to result in victory for the ministers who advised its use. Melbourne, therefore, was censured for having advised the Queen to dissolve parliament instead of resigning. For it was argued that, by resigning, he would have saved the Queen from the humiliation of defeat and, moreover, ensured that the next general election should be a confirmation of the Queen's choice of minister. Few, and least of all the victorious Peel, were radical enough to see with equanimity the Queen's minister roundly rejected by the electorate. Indeed, the fact that this had happened was not taken as a reason for the Queen's dismissal of that minister. Melbourne resigned not after his defeat at the general election in June but after his defeat by the new House of Commons at the end of August, and he was blamed not for retaining office against the wishes of the electorate but for retaining office against the wishes of the old House of Commons.

The possibility of electoral defeat seemed, at first, greatly to increase the influence of the Commons over the

King's ministers. For, as dissolution after defeat in the Commons was no longer practicable, defeat came to be regarded as normally requiring the resignation of ministers and the choice of new ones more acceptable to the Commons. Defeat in the Commons was sometimes the aftermath of defeat in a general election, but this was still not always so. This ascendancy of the Commons did not survive the second Reform Act, and in any case could not have survived the tighter party organisation which followed in the wake of a larger electorate. As the House of Commons came to be more and more fixed in the party divisions evident at the time of its election, so it became farcical to pretend that a government defeated at a general election had any chance of escaping defeat in the new House, and it became correspondingly unlikely that a government which decisively won a general election would be defeated during the lifetime of the House then elected. It was this development which finally took from the King the choice of his prime minister, for it now became expedient — and indeed necessary — that the prime minister should be chosen at the same time as the House of Commons was chosen, and that he should be chosen not in conformity with the wishes of the Commons but in conformity with the result of the general election which constituted the Commons. This was a shift of power not from King to Commons but from both to the electorate. Disraeli's decision to resign in December 1868, immediately after his defeat at the first general election after the second Reform Act, and without meeting the new House of Commons, may perhaps be defended as the open acceptance of a situation which had been only masked since 1832. Nevertheless, his decision was still regretted by constitutionalists because it symbolized the final overthrow of the old balance of the constitution by the intrusion of a new element, the electorate.

Disraeli's resignation was in accordance with a new

theory which, after the second Reform Act, came finally to supersede the old : that the choice of ministers depended neither on King nor on Commons but on the electorate, and that a general election was an appeal to the electorate to decide between two possible sets of ministers, between two parties and two party programmes, both equally acceptable to the King. This was the end of the King's real choice of prime minister, the end of the period in which the King chose his servants when he wished and not at the same time as the electorate chose the House of Commons, the end even of the period in which his choice was restricted only by the desirability of having ministers who were acceptable to the Commons. Just as this development was, for the King, part of the great metamorphosis which took him out of politics, so it was, for his ministers, part of the process which turned them into a reflection of the larger part of the electorate at the moment of election.

By 1832 only the first step in this process had been taken. The emergence of a prime minister as leader of a smaller and stronger cabinet meant that the King usually, though not invariably, allowed the prime minister to name most of his colleagues, and that an increasing number of members of the cabinet were normally chosen at the same time. This development had not much affected the relation between the Commons and the King's servants — except in so far as it helped the King's servants to manage the Commons — for the choice of prime minister was still the King's. The King made his choice independently of the electorate's choice of the Commons, and at a different time : a general election remained an appeal from the King on behalf of ministers he had previously chosen and was not followed by a change of ministry. The Commons had no say in the King's choice and their influence on it was as indirect as it had been at any time since 1660 : the king might find his task easier if he chose ministers acceptable to the House but he was not in any way bound to do so. On the other hand, the Commons had more say in the retention of ministries in 1832 than they had done in the past : the decline of patronage meant that the King was less likely either to be able prematurely to change the House for the benefit of his ministers or to obtain a more favourable House at a normal general election. This inevitably increased the Commons' chances of being able to secure the dismissal or force the resignation of ministers they disliked, but even so, it was not yet universally admitted that defeat in the House compelled resignation, and in fact defeat was not always followed by the formation of a new administration. The Commons were, then, in 1832 at the beginning of a period when their influence on the King's choice of ministers, though it remained indirect, was in practice larger than ever before. But the life of the King's servants remained, in 1832 and for some time afterwards, normally distinct from the life of the Commons, and it was indeed because this was so that, as far as influence over ministers was concerned, the Commons and not the electorate reaped the first advantage of the Reform Act.

CHAPTER VI

CONCLUSION

THE need for co-operation between King and Commons grew more urgent in proportion as the Commons' ascendancy in parliament made them more equally matched. The need was present before 1660, and the reigns of the later Stuarts only emphasized the inadequacy of the solution offered both by the legislation of the Long Parliament in 1641, and by the Restoration settlement, which made no advance on it. The legislation of 1641 was supplemented in the years after 1689. By 1716 the King could not, without infringing statute law, legislate outside parliament or set aside Acts of Parliament, and he could not, without parliamentary sanction, supplement his ordinary revenue by taxation or maintain a standing army. Moreover, the King's fundamental prerogative in relation to the House of Commons, the summoning and dissolving of parliament, had been to some extent curtailed by statute, while the coming of regular annual sessions, in the wake of financial needs, had made the Commons almost as continuous a part of the constitution as the King. On the other hand, the King retained his extra-parliamentary position as head and sole constitutor of the executive government, and this position even seemed to be fortified by the coming of regular parliaments, with a life distinct from that of the King's ministers. Thus, by 1716, legislation, combined with the failure of the Commons to control the King's choice of ministers, had provided a legal framework for the relations between King and Commons.

Upon this legal framework were built, after 1716, the constitutional conventions which made possible a working relationship between King and Commons. The two vital conventions were those which concerned the life and the composition of the Commons : the first gave the Commons an existence more regular than and clearly separated from that of the King's ministers ; the second ensured that the necessary co-operation between King and Commons, which statute could not provide, should be based on an overlap of personnel between them.

Both conventions were precarious. The first depended on the King's not using his prerogative of dissolution until the statutory maximum life of parliament was drawing to a close ; the second depended on the Commons' not pressing their desire for independence so far as to exclude all placemen unconditionally from their House. For this reason, the equilibrium maintained in the period 1716–83 was an uneasy one. The Commons perhaps valued the equilibrium more than the King, because they had climbed up to it on his losses. But the Commons were, for this reason, even more conscious of the sacrifice of their principles entailed by the second convention, and the very nature of this convention emphasized that they, unlike the King, had no source of power outside the parliamentary balance. Accordingly, the danger that the King might unduly intrude into the House of Commons his powers as head of the executive, in order to weight the parliamentary balance in his favour, was the constant pre-occupation of the eighteenth-century House of Commons. It is perhaps only in retrospect that the Commons seem more anxious than they need have been. It is of course true that the King's efforts to win over individual members of the Commons was a sign that he was on the defensive, but even if the Commons had acknowledged this they could hardly have acquiesced in the process. Even the first convention, the very basis of the Commons' strength, did not quite reassure them, since, after all, the Septennial Act left the King legally free to dissolve parliament at any time within its maximum life. Moreover, the fact that the Septennial Act was a measure favoured by the government, and introduced into the House of Lords, at first obscured its value to the Commons.

There can be no doubt that it was the Septennial convention which elevated the Commons to a position of sufficient independence to form an equal part of the constitutional trio of King, Lords, and Commons and so, in Gibbon's words, 'maintain the peace and stability of government'. It was, too, the Septennial convention which supported the Commons' occasional claims to supremacy, not only within the parliamentary balance, over King and Lords, but also outside it, over the electorate and over the King's choice of ministers. For the septennial general elections which produced the parliaments of the period 1716–83 were not connected in theory with changes of administration, as they were not connected in time with them. The House of Commons was chosen by the electorate, and when chosen was free of the electorate ; ministers were chosen by the King, and did not enjoy similar advantages either of regularity or of freedom. In practice, the onus of working together lay with the ministers rather than with the Commons, and ministers stood or fell by their ability to manage the Commons. If they failed to do so, at least until the next general election, it was they, rather than the Commons, who were likely to be changed.

For this reason, the implications of the Septennial convention themselves increased the value of the second convention, for it was the second convention which preserved the equilibrium by providing the King and his ministers with a method of influencing the Commons without overriding them. This method, the 'patronage system', not only weakened the Commons in relation to the King but also averted open conflict between them. It ensured that a general election produced a House of Commons which was in the main well disposed towards the King's ministers, and although it was not able to ensure that this friendly disposition lasted, it provided assistance towards this end. The House of Commons found it difficult to attack this method because it was based on a conflict of interest between the House and its members. Thus the House was in a sense paralysed : in spite of its Place Bills and its abuse of placemen it continued to be influenced and its members continued to be placed. David Hume believed that this conflict of interest provided the key to the 'paradox' of the parliamentary balance. 'The share of power allotted by our constitution to the House of Commons, is so great, that it absolutely commands all the other parts of the government.' The reason why the Commons had, nevertheless, not overwhelmed both King and Lords was to be found in the conflict of interest which separated the House and its members, for this conflict, grounded in human nature, kept the system of influence alive and therefore ensured stability of government. 'I answer', said Hume, 'that the interest of the body is here restrained by that of the individuals, and that the House of Commons stretches not its power, because such an usurpation would be contrary to the interest of the majority of its members. The crown has so many offices at its disposal, that, when assisted by the honest and disinterested part of the House, it will always command the resolutions of the whole, so far, at least, as to preserve the ancient constitution from danger. We may, therefore, give to this influence what name we please ; we may call it by the invidious appellations of *corruption* and *dependence* ; but some degree and some kind of it are inseparable from the very nature of the constitution, and necessary to the preservation of our mixed government.'

The decline in the volume of crown patronage between

1784 and 1832 was not less effective because it was not
the result of a resolving of the conflict of interest between
the House and its members. In consequence of the decline,
the general elections of the early nineteenth century were
less easily won by the King's ministers and the Commons
when elected were less easily managed by them. At the
same time, the Septennial convention was not uniformly
observed by the King, who began to apply the theory that
dissolution was the most precious prerogative of the crown
at the beginning of a period in which it was ceasing to
be practically expedient to do so. The Commons' greater
independence was to some extent offset by an increase in
the power of the cabinet, but although this development
strengthened the government in relation to the Commons,
it weakened the King in relation to his ministers, for it
emphasized the value of their ability to manage the Commons with less help from his patronage. So, before the
passing of any Reform Bill, the relation between King
and Commons was being transformed. Influence was no
longer enough to throw a bridge between them; the Commons were gaining in power and independence at the
expense of the King and the King's ministers were doing
the same. The Reform Act of 1832, like the decline of
influence before it, weakened the King both in relation to
the Commons and in relation to his ministers; but its most
radical effect was to increase the power and independence
of the electorate. It was this, the advent of a new kind of
electorate, and not the increase in the power of the Commons, which finally destroyed the old parliamentary balance. For the balance lost all meaning when the electorate
came, at the same time, to choose both the House of
Commons and the King's ministers and to bind them
almost indissolubly together. The destruction of the
parliamentary balance was not accepted in 1832, nor was
it fully operative until, after 1867, the electorate was
organized into fixed parties. The 1832 Reform Act

seemed, therefore, to increase the power of the Commons more than it did in fact, and in the short golden age after 1832 the Commons, though doomed to be mastered by the electorate, were more clearly masters of the King and the King's ministers than they had ever been before.

PARLIAMENTS AND MINISTERS: 1716–1832

Parliaments : Date of Summons and Dissolution	Ministers : Date of Appointment of First Lord of the Treasury	
March 1715–March 1722	May 1715	Carlisle
	October 1715	Walpole
	April 1717	Stanhope
	March 1718	Sunderland
	April 1721	Walpole
May 1722–August 1727		
November 1727–April 1734		
June 1734–April 1741		
June 1741–June 1747	February 1742	Wilmington
	August 1743	Pelham
	February 1746	Bath
	February 1746	Pelham
August 1747–April 1754	March 1754	Newcastle
May 1754–March 1761	November 1756	Devonshire
	June 1757	Waldegrave
	June 1757	Newcastle
May 1761–March 1768	May 1762	Bute
	May 1763	Grenville
	July 1765	Rockingham
	August 1766	Grafton
	December 1767	Grafton
May 1768–September 1774	January 1770	North
November 1774– September 1780		
October 1780–March 1784	March 1782	Rockingham
	July 1782	Shelburne
	April 1783	Portland
	December 1783	Pitt
May 1784–June 1790		
August 1790–May 1796		
July 1796–June 1802	March 1801	Addington
August 1802–October 1806	May 1804	Pitt
	January 1806	Grenville

Parliaments : Date of Summons and Dissolution	Ministers : Date of Appointment of First Lord of the Treasury	
December 1806–April 1807	March 1807	Portland
June 1807–September 1812	September 1807	Perceval
	May 1812	Liverpool
November 1812–June 1818		
August 1818–February 1820		
April 1820–June 1826		
July 1826–July 1830	March 1827	Canning
	August 1827	Goderich
	January 1828	Wellington
September 1830–April 1831	November 1830	Grey
June 1831–December 1832	May 1832	Grey

MEMBERS OF PARLIAMENT VACATING SEATS ON APPOINTMENT TO OFFICE [1]

Parliament	Number of Vacations	Number of Vacations followed by Re-election	Number of Vacations not followed by Re-election	Number of Changes of Administration
1715–22	107	82	25	5
1722–7	62	46	16	—
1727–34	63	50	13	—
1734–41	54	39	15	—
1741–7	85	71	14	4
1747–54	43	32	11	1[2]
1754–61	95	74	21	3
1761–8	124	102	22	5
1768–74	61	47	14	1
1774–80	51	38	13	—
1780–4	83	75	8	4
1784–90	42	23	19	—
1790–6	41	29	12	—
1796–1802	55	44	11	1
1802–6	73	58	15	2
1806–7	21	18	3	1
1807–12	48	31	17	2
1812–18	37	23	14	—
1818–20	14	11	3	—
1820–6	30	20	10	—
1826–30	58	49	9	3
1830–1	24	22	2	1
1831–2	6	6	—	1

[1] Excluding members who accepted the office of Steward of the Chiltern Hundreds or similar offices.

[2] On p. 98 this parliament is counted as one which saw no changes of administration, for there were no re-elections between the 'change of administration' on Pelham's death in March 1754 and the dissolution of parliament in April.

MEMBERS OF PARLIAMENT WHO VACATED SEATS ON APPOINTMENT TO OFFICE DURING NORTH'S ADMINISTRATION, 1770–82

	Vacation followed by Re-election	Vacation not followed by Re-election
1. 1770–4 (from North's appointment to the dissolution of parliament)	38	14
2. 1774–80	38	13
3. 1780–2 (from the opening of parliament to North's resignation)	7	3
Total	83	30

ANALYSIS OF RE-ELECTIONS

	Ministers	Junior Ministers	Civil Servants, Paymasters, Legal Officers	Household and Court Officials, Sinecures, Miscellaneous
1	Chancellor of the Exchequer Attorney General Solicitor General (2)	Treasury Board (5) Admiralty Board (3) Board of Trade (7)	Clerk of Ordnance Clerk of Deliveries, Ordnance Treasurer of Navy Vice-Treasurer, Ireland (2) Justice of Welsh counties Judge of High Court of Admiralty	Comptroller of Household Vice-Chamberlain of Household (2) Cofferer of Household Treasurer of Chamber Groom of Bedchamber (2) Keeper of King's Private Roads (2) Remembrancer of Exchequer, Scotland Governor of Isle of Wight Secretary, Leeward Islands

Appendix C

	Ministers	Junior Ministers	Civil Servants, Paymasters, Legal Officers	Household and Court Officials, Sinecures, Miscellaneous
2	Secretary of State Secretary at War Attorney General Solicitor General	Treasury Board (2) Admiralty Board (4) Board of Trade (4)	Store Keeper, Ordnance Treasurer of Navy Vice-Treasurer, Ireland Welsh Justices (2)	Comptroller of Household Cofferer of Household (2) Clerk Comptroller of Household (2) Clerk of Household Treasurer of Chamber Groom of Bedchamber (2) Attorney General, Duchy of Lancaster Surveyor General of Works Surveyor General of Land Revenue Writer of Tallies Commissary General of Musters Warden of Cinque Ports Lord Advocate, Scotland Keeper of Signet, Scotland (3)
3	Secretary of State	Treasury Board (1) Board of Trade (3)		Receiver General of Land Revenue, N. Wales Auditor of Land Revenue, N. Wales

APPENDIX D

MEMBERS OF PARLIAMENT APPOINTED TO OFFICE AND RE-ELECTED AT THE BEGINNING OF A NEW ADMINISTRATION

	Ministers	Junior Ministers	Civil Servants	Household, etc.
Walpole, April–June 1721	Chancellor of the Exchequer	Treasury Board (1)		
Pelham, February–April 1746		Admiralty Board (1) Board of Trade (1)	Chief Store Keeper, Ordnance Clerk of Deliveries, Ordnance Vice-Treasurer, Ireland Commissioner of Navy	Groom of Bedchamber
Bute, May–July 1762	Chancellor of the Exchequer Secretary of State	Treasury Board (1)	Treasurer of Ordnance Treasurer of Navy	Treasurer of Chamber
North, January–March 1770	Chancellor of the Exchequer	Treasury Board (1) Admiralty Board (2)	Treasurer of Navy Vice-Treasurer, Ireland	Vice-Chamberlain of Household
Rockingham, March–May 1782	Chancellor of the Exchequer Secretary of State Secretary at War (2) Attorney General	Treasury Board (3) Admiralty Board (4)	Surveyor General, Ordnance Treasurer of Navy Paymaster of Forces	Comptroller of Household Vice-Admiral, Scotland
Pitt, December 1783– February 1784	Chancellor of the Exchequer Secretary at War Attorney General	Treasury Board (4) Admiralty Board (4)	Treasurer of Navy Paymaster of Forces	Secretary, Chelsea Hospital Surveyor General of Land Revenue

APPENDIX E

PLACEMEN ELECTED AT THE
GENERAL ELECTION OF 1780

(*Note*. This is a table of *placemen elected*, and not of *places held*, in order to show the potential numerical support for the government in the new House of Commons. Placemen who held more than one office are marked with an asterisk. Military and naval officers holding a civil place are denoted under it, and other plural placemen are shown under the most important place they held. The information is based, in the main, on the *Royal Kalendar* for 1781 : a small margin of error cannot be excluded.)

1. *Ministers and Law Officers*
    *Chancellor of the Exchequer
    *Secretary of State
    *Secretary at War
    *Attorney General
    Solicitor General

2. *Junior Ministers*
    ***Treasury Board : 4 (of whom 3 held other places)
    ***Admiralty Board : 6 (of whom 3 held other places)
    ***Board of Trade : 5 (of whom 3 held other places)

3. *Civil Servants and Paymasters*
    **2 Secretaries to the Treasury (both holding other places)
    Secretary to Chancellor of the Exchequer
    *Secretary to the Admiralty
    Under-Secretary of State
    *Surveyor General of Ordnance
    Storekeeper of Ordnance
    Clerk of Ordnance
    Secretary to Master General of Ordnance
    *Paymaster General
    Deputy to Paymaster General
    Treasurer of Navy
    2 Vice-Treasurers, Ireland
    Chancellor of Exchequer, Ireland

*Accountant of Sixpenny Receiver's Office
Envoy to Court of Dresden

4. *Legal Officers*
   Counsel to Admiralty and Navy
   Counsel to Board of Trade
   Advocate General to Army
   Solicitor General, Scotland
   *Lord Advocate, Scotland
   2 Welsh Justices
   Justice of Chester
   Attorney General of N. Wales Circuit
   Master in Chancery
   *Clerk of Crown in Chancery

5. *Household and Court Officials*
   *Comptroller of Household
   Vice-Chamberlain of Household
   *Cofferer of Household
   *Comptroller of King's Wardrobe
   *Treasurer of Chamber
   *Deputy Treasurer of Chamber
   *Lord of Bedchamber
   *Groom of Bedchamber
   Gentleman of Privy Chamber
   Clerk Comptroller, Board of Green Cloth
   3 Clerks of Board of Green Cloth
   Surveyor General of Crown Lands
   *Master of Buckhounds
   *Heritable Usher of White Rod
   Surveyor of King's Private Roads
   Joint Printer to King
   Procurator General to King
   *Paymaster, Board of Works
   Surveyor, Board of Works
   *Secretary and Comptroller to Queen
   Solicitor General to Queen
   *Groom of Bedchamber to Duke of Gloucester
   Receiver General, Duchy of Cornwall
   Attorney General, Duchy of Cornwall
   Vice-Warden of Stannaries of Cornwall
   Secretary to Order of Thistle

6. *Sinecures, Keepers and Rangers of Forests, Governors, Miscellaneous*
        Teller of Exchequer
      *Auditor of Imprest
      *Keeper of Rockingham Forest
      Out Ranger, Windsor Forest
      *Deputy Ranger, Whittlebury Forest
      Deputy Ranger, Phoenix Park
      *Chief Justice in Eyre, Forests South of Trent
      Chief Justice in Eyre, Forests North of Trent
      2 Lords Register, Scotland
      *Clerk of Hanaper, Ireland
      Conservator of Scots Privileges in Netherlands
  ***6 Lords Lieutenant (of whom 3 held other places)
 ****10 Recorders (of whom 4 held other places)
      *Governor of Jersey
      *Governor of Portsmouth
      *Governor of Hull
      *Lieutenant Governor of Hull
      *Governor of Tinmouth
      *Governor of Fort William
      *Governor of Upnor Castle
      Captain of Sangate Castle
      Vice-Admiral of Shetland and Orkneys
      Chamberlain of Fife
    *2 Directors of Greenwich Hospital (of whom one held another place)
    *3 Elder Brothers of Trinity House (of whom one held another place)
      *Governor of Chelsea Hospital
      President of Misericordia Hospital
      Trustee of British Museum

7. *Army and Navy officers not holding another place*
      43 (30 Army, 13 Navy)

THE PARLIAMENTARY FUNCTION OF PATRONAGE

Letter to Lorth North on his Re-election into the House of Commons, by a Member of the late Parliament. London, *1780* (Bodleian Library, *Godwyn Pamphlets*, vol. 938)

(THE premature general election of September 1780 followed the success, on 6 April, of Dunning's Resolution 'that the influence of the Crown has increased, is increasing, and ought to be diminished', and the failure, later in the month, of the attempt to restrain the King from dissolving parliament until the resolution had been implemented by legislation. The *Letter* points out that in spite of the protestations of the economical reformers, their attack on the King's influence was in fact followed by an attack on the King's prerogative. This alienated many country gentlemen who had voted for Dunning and was, in the opinion of the author of the *Letter*, one of the reasons for the government's electoral successes. Against this background, the author discusses the place of influence in the constitution.)

. . . I am no advocate for a slavish and mercenary House of Commons; but I am ready to profess myself a friend to royal influence in the state. The ideas are perfectly distinct and separate; so much so, that when influence and corruption are confounded with one another, and used as synonymous expressions, I cannot give credit to mankind for such a degree of stupidity, as to believe them unable, and therefore must suppose them unwilling, to discern the difference. . . . That influence, to a certain degree, and under proper limitations, ought to exist, is admitted fairly by those who are now for its diminution; in all their speeches they fairly state, that the Crown has *too much* influence. Their arguments all go to shew an approbation of it, if kept within proper bounds; they are ready to recognize and justify it as a principle of Whiggism. Even Mr. Hume, who has sometimes been supposed to be no great favourer of those principles, has directly opposed and answered the position in Lord Bolingbroke's Dissertation on Parties 'that the dependence of Parliament, in *every degree* is an infringement of British liberty.' Mr. Hume thinks, that it would have been more prudent in the management of the argument, for the country party of that time to have made some concessions, and have only examined what was the proper degree of this dependence, beyond which it became dangerous to liberty. He argues the necessity of influence, from the danger which would arise to our constitution from the excess of power entrusted to the House of Commons. . . .

It is exceedingly difficult, not only to ascertain the degree which ought to exist, and fix the proper medium, but also to find words to describe the nature of influence precisely, though it is very easy to distinguish it from corruption. It arises from the patronage which necessarily resides in the Crown, which cannot be taken away from it without abolishing the functions of a supreme executive magistrate and destroying the office of King. . . . From thence it comes, that the Crown is possessed of such a patronage. It was not originally given for the purpose of creating an influence in the legislature, but that influence was an unavoidable, and, as we have seen, a beneficial consequence of it. . . .

It is much easier to assert and say, that the fact is too notorious to be disputed, and that everyone is a daily witness to the excessive influence of the Crown, than to state with any degree of candour, intelligence and precision, how far the increase of influence from any given period (for instance, from the Revolution), arising from the augmentation of our fleets and armies, and of our national debt, is greater or less, than the defalcation of it by various means and circumstances ; some of them imputable to accident, as flowing from unforeseen political events, and the changes incidental to the progress of time ; and some the effect of design, resulting from the deliberate intention of the legislature and prescribed by positive institution. Of this latter sort, are all those statutory provisions for the diminution of influence. Acts of Parliament, creating disabilities in certain officers of the Crown to sit in the House of Commons. . . . Besides these disabling statutes, it is to be observed, that the legislature has enacted that so often as any member shall accept an office under the Crown (excepting in the army and navy), it shall vacate his seat in Parliament, though it is not one of those offices which disqualify him to be re-elected. . . .

But, instead of following up their resolutions with some specific proposal on that head . . . instead of aiming their next blow at the influence of the Crown, they at once abandoned the ground on which they were triumphant, in order to make an attack on another subject, totally different in its nature, namely, the prerogative of the Crown.

A motion was made, *to address the Crown not to dissolve the Parliament or prorogue the present session, until proper measures had been taken to diminish the influence, and correct the other abuses complained of by the petitions of the people.*

This was entering a new field of battle . . . no complaints had been made by the people, no dissatisfaction had been expressed by Parliament on account of prerogative ; on the contrary, it was said to have been already sufficiently curtailed, to have been sunk almost into oblivion (quotes Burke, *Thoughts on the Causes of the Present Discontents*, in support of this statement). . . .

I shall not misspend my time in proving, that the lawful prerogative of the Crown was attacked by this motion. For although the power of the Crown to dissolve the Parliament was not denied, but rather recognized, by this motion ; yet it is too clear to stand in need of any argument, that any interference of the House in the matter of its own dissolution, carries so much authority with it, that its advice or recommendations amounts in effect to little less than assumption of that prerogative. . . .

INFRINGEMENT OF THE SEPTENNIAL CONVENTION

Extract from the *Annual Register*, 1806, p. 262.

(Grenville's administration, formed after Pitt's death in January 1806, advised and obtained the dissolution of parliament in October. The new parliament met in December and was in its turn dissolved, on the advice of Grenville's successor Portland, in April 1807. The two dissolutions were criticized on the same grounds : that, unless a special emergency existed, a new administration was not justified in seeking to strengthen itself by asking for a new parliament.)

The only measure of the new ministry, that falls under our notice in the course of the present year, is the dissolution of parliament, on which we confess that we cannot bestow our commendation. Even the advocates of this whig administration, we apprehend, must admit, that in this measure they sacrificed to temporary expediency the permanent interests of the constitution. The crown has unquestionably the right of dissolving parliament. But from the composition of that assembly, the exercise of this right tends infallibly to increase the influence of ministers in the house of commons, and, therefore, were it ever to become the usual practice of our government, for those in office to dissolve parliaments, when not constituted to their liking, those assemblies, influenced by the terrors of a premature dissolution, which is always inconvenient and expensive to their members, would lose all spirit of liberty or resistance, and become the tame and servile instruments of court. If septennial parliaments are found to be of too long duration, it would be better at once to revive the triennial act, than palliate the evil by a remedy, which, every time it is repeated, adds to the influence of the crown over the representatives of the people. We are not ignorant that particular situations and emergencies call for this exertion of the prerogative ; but we know of no sufficient reason to justify the advice to exercise it on the present occasion. There was no difference of opinion between the two houses of parliament. Peace, it is true, had not been obtained ; but the causes, that had led to a rupture of the negotiation, were unknown to the public, when parliament was dissolved ; and judging from past experience, there could be no apprehension of too strong a disposition to peace in the existing house of commons, or of any reluctance in its members to concur in the most expensive measures for the vigorous prosecution of the war.

The returns to the new parliament were such as greatly to add to the weight and influence of the friends of administration in the house of commons.

INDEX

Index

Fox, Charles James—*contd.*
on Montesquieu, 83 n.
on Commons and ministers, 130
Fundamental laws, 28-30, 41

General Elections :
theory and function of, 91, 93, 113-14, 135-7, 139, 143-6
timing of, 76-82
use of King's name at, 136, 137
issues at, 135-6
and Reform Act, 110-12, 136-7
difficulties of, after 1784, 128, 136-7, 145
individual elections :
1681, 44 n.
1715, 40, 43
1727, 38, 77 n.
1741, 94 n.
1747, 38, 77 n., 78
1754, 149 n.
1774, 38, 39 n., 45 n., 50, 78, 99
1780, 38, 39, 39 n., 77 n., 78, 156
1784, 5, 45 n., 78, 79, 80, 110, 133-5
1796, 77, 79
1802, 77, 79
1806, 78, 80, 159
1807, 78, 80, 81, 159
1812, 78, 80, 81-2
1818, 77, 79
1820, 78
1830, 78, 79, 135
1831, 78, 136
1835, 79, 135, 137
1837, 135, 137
1841, 79, 135, 137
1868, 138
See also Dissolution
George I (1660-1727), 4, 38, 72, 77 n., 121, 124
creation of peers by, 65
and peerage bill, 66
George II (1683-1760), 63, 74, 75, 121, 122
George III (1738-1820), 39 n., 74, 75, 92, 101 n., 102, 122
and general election of 1784, 5
and choice of ministers, 124, 128, 129, 132, 133-4
George IV (1762-1830), 79, 108, 129, 132
Gibbon, Edward (1737-94), 143
Gladstone, William Ewart (1809-1898), 103

Glanville, John (1586-1661), 12 n.
Glyn, John (1722-79), 45 n.
Goderich, Viscount. *See under* Robinson
Grand Remonstrance (1641), 28, 155
Grenville, George (1712-70), 147
Grenville, George Nugent Temple, 2nd Earl Temple, 1st Marquis of Buckingham (1753-1813), 133 n.
Grenville, William Wyndham, Baron (1759-1834), 129
and dissolution of 1806, 81, 159
dismissal of (1807), 131, 132
Grey, Charles, 2nd Earl (1764-1845), 129, 132, 136
Grimstone, Sir Harbottle (1603-85), 81
Guilford, 2nd Earl of. *See under* North

Halifax, 1st Marquis of. *See under* Savile
Hanmer, Sir Thomas (1677-1746), 4
Harley, Robert, 1st Earl of Oxford (1661-1724), 66
Hatsell, John (1743-1820), 56
Hawkesbury, Baron. *See under* Jenkinson
Heron, Sir Robert (1765-1854), 62 n.
Herries, John Charles (1778-1855), 129
History of Lord North's Administration, The (1781), 38, 39 n.
House of Commons. *See* Commons.
House of Lords. *See* Lords
Howard, Charles, 3rd Earl of Carlisle (1674-1738), 147
Hume, David (1711-76)
on relation between members and constituents, 45
on influence, 88, 89, 144, 156, 157
Hussey, Sir Edward (d. ? 1707), 54

Impeachment, 86, 115-16
Influence. *See under* Placemen
Inglis, Sir Robert Harry (1786-1855), 108
Instructions to members, 2, 43-6.
See also Constituents

James I (1566-1625), 18
James II (1633-1701), 3, 12 n., 17, 18, 25
and borough charters, 15, 21

163

Index

THE END

Printed in Great Britain by
Lowe and Brydone (Printers) Limited, London, N.W.10

DATE

HIGHSMITH 45-220

PRINTED IN U.S.A.